Bluffs to Bayous

One man's solo kayak expedition down the Mississippi and Atchafalaya Rivers

BYRON CURTIS

Great Rivers Printing
Prescott, Wisconsin
(715) 262-4848

Front and back cover photos by Wendi Curtis
All interior photos by the author.

ISBN 0-9740152-0-2

Manufactured in the United States of America
First Edition/First Printing

DEDICATION

I dedicate this book to my best friend. She is always by my side in times of sorrow and joy and in times of riches and great need. Her unconditional love and generosity are an encouragement to me. Wendi Curtis, my wonderful wife, I thank you for all that you are and mean to me. I dedicate this book to you. I love you sweetheart.

SPECIAL THANKS

I thank God for the strength and endurance to complete this trip.

Thanks, Isaac, for letting your dad go for 42 days.

I thank my mom, sisters, brother, and their families for their support.

I appreciate my in-laws here in Wisconsin for helping my wife and son while I was away on the river.

Thanks also go to my good friends, Mike and Linda Shilts, for their insight and support.

I also thank Jerry Knight and Sally Zastrow for the great poems they wrote, which are printed in this book.

I appreciate the many hours Steve and Penny Peterson contributed to editing and proofreading this book.

Special thanks go out to all my friends at the Prescott School District. Their encouragement alone was enough to float me down the river. I will never forget the wonderful send-off they gave me.

And to the community of Prescott, a great little river town full of good people, I say thank you.

PREFACE

The intrigue of adventure tugs at my heart and mind. The waters that surround my homes have always fascinated me. As a young boy living in west-central Wisconsin, I spent days upon days fishing, playing in, and wandering the banks of the Wolf River. As a young adult, the rivers of Alaska provided heart-pounding salmon fishing. The Platte River of Wyoming and its reservoirs afforded me endless hours of paddling pleasure. And now the Mississippi River lures me to explore its bluffs and mysterious backwaters. From my earliest years, I have been attracted to streams, rivers, lakes and even the world's oceans.

Late in the year of 1999, a job opportunity brought my family from the state of Wyoming to my home state of Wisconsin—to a small town called Prescott. How fortunate I am that this historic community was purposefully established on the confluence of the Mississippi and St. Croix Rivers. Upon moving here, it was not long before I loaded up my kayak and drove a half-mile to a local boat launch. Little did I know that this first paddle would lead me to a fascinating journey on the great Mississippi River.

During my two years of living and working in Prescott, I have become more and more interested in paddling the river. I earned my certification as a kayak instructor and teach classes on the Mississippi and St. Croix Rivers through our local Community Education Program. These opportunities give me more time on the river—time to appreciate its beauty and wonder.

It is January 2001 when I begin thinking about the possibility of undertaking an expedition somewhere in the world. I contemplate circumnavigating large islands, exploring cold oceans and crossing endless seas. Then it dawns on me; I live only a half-mile from a great expedition—paddling the Mississippi River to the Gulf of Mexico.

Hesitantly, I introduce this journey to my wife, Wendi, and my son, Isaac. Wendi is, as always, very positive from the first mention of it. She encourages me to gather more details and explore the possibility. Isaac doesn't say much at first. Later, when I announce that I am seriously thinking about paddling to the Gulf, Isaac responds, not with arrogance, but sincerity, "Dad you won't go!" He just doesn't think I will take on such an enormous challenge. At this point, I decide to be a man of my word—to do what I say I will do. In March, I begin seriously searching out information, as much as I can find about the Mississippi River, from books, magazines, the Internet, others who have completed the trip, and from a paddling group that lives much farther south on the river.

As word of my adventure seeps out, several people tell me that they would love to take a journey like this. So in some ways, I am taking on this endeavor for them—for all those who want to, but never get the chance. My dad also loved streams and rivers. We spent endless hours together wandering through them, whether we were hunting, fishing, or trapping. Even though my dad, whom I greatly love and respect, is passed away, I embark on this voyage for him.

I decide early on that my departure date will be September 4, 2001. I am hoping that this time of the year will offer me moderate temperatures, stable and temperate weather conditions, fewer insects, and less boat traffic. I am left with about five months to plan, prepare, and organize all I will need to make this dream a reality.

My purpose for this journey is not to race or to visit tourist attractions inside the towns; I can do that from my car. From the seat of my kayak or from the river's banks, I want to meet the people who live, work and play on the river.

I'm not interested in starting at the beginning, at Lake Itasca and finishing at Mile Zero, beyond New Orleans. I want to start where I live, work and play—in Prescott, Wisconsin. I want to see what the river sees, hear what the river hears and end where the river ends—the Gulf of Mexico. I want this trip to be purely a "river" trip.

One thing I knew as a boy and still know now as a man, I truly love the waters. Paddling them stirs an adventurous spirit deep within my soul. Each new stroke of the paddle brings new sights and sounds that eventually lead to this book, *Bluffs to Bayous*.

ONE MAN'S DREAM

Deep inside this man had a dream;
One man, one kayak, a winning team!
All alone down a river so large,
With sailboats, ships and an occasional barge.

Stroke by stroke he leaves his home,
Down the River to the Gulf he'll roam.
Spending nights along the shore,
Knowing the next day holds even more.

With the Gulf Coast as his quest,
There's not much time for him to rest.
As his supplies dwindle down,
He'll have to make a trip to town.

Though he's challenged, he shows no fear,
Because his goal is getting near.
His friends and family pray each day,
That he will safely go his way.

We wish you well Byron, on your way,
As you start you journey here today.
May you always feel God's presence near,
With the sights you see and sounds you hear!

Jerry Knight 9/4/01

THE EARLY YEARS

"Don't panic! Don't panic!" I yelled to my friend who was sinking in swirling waters over his head.

We were about twelve years old, I guess, and always looking for excitement down by the river. We felt like we had struck gold when someone gave us an old wooden rowboat. It was our ticket to great adventure on the river.

We spent most of the morning dragging that old wooden boat to Mitten Bank.

Mitten Bank was a high bank overlooking the Wolf River where my neighbor lady Gram and I would sit while fishing. Gram would get a fish hooked and let me crank it up the high bank. It was only about a hundred yards or so from my house, but it seemed worlds away. What fun for a five-year-old boy.

One cold day, while Gram and I were fishing, I dropped one of the mittens I was wearing—the kind grandmas knit for kids. It caught on a briar bush twenty feet down the bank. There it hung, two feet above the surface of the water. I thought I had lost it forever. But never fear; Gram was an expert with that old fishing rod. On her second or third cast, she snagged my little blue mitten and cranked it back to the safety of my small hand that, by then, had turned red from the cold. I sure had some fun times fishing with Gram from Mitten Bank.

My friend and I stopped at the top of Mitten Bank and took a peek at the water below. It was April or May and the river was swollen from heavy spring runoff. *Perfect timing*, we thought.

We edged the craft over the side of the bank to the water's edge. Grabbing sticks for control, we pushed off from the bank into the fast-moving current. We had no clue how far or where we were going. Getting the boat into the water as soon as possible was all that mattered.

The boat moved along at a good clip, pushed around by eddies and whirlpools, created by the high water. We bumped into fallen trees and floating logs as we made our way down the swollen river. We thought things were going pretty well for a couple of boys who knew nothing about river navigation.

Surprisingly, a cold feeling crept up around our ankles. The boat was leaking. Here we were, proud captains of this old wooden boat, peacefully drifting down a flooded river, and now it was sinking less than a half-mile from where we put in.

With no life jacket to keep him afloat, my friend leaped into the icy, swirling water. I saw his head go under and then finally pop back up. I yelled, "Don't panic! Don't panic! Swim for shore!" The old wooden boat became very unsteady as it filled with water. I had no choice; it was my turn to jump. The cold water jolted me. I dog paddled to shore, where my shivering friend was waiting. We made it alive, but lost our pride and joy—the old wooden boat.

This experience did not dampen my desire to be on the water. When my older sister came home for the summer, she told me of a friend from college who had a raft for sale. *Another opportunity to be on the water.* I paid my sister the hard-earned cash for the raft, and in two long, very long, weeks, my sister brought it home for me.

I unfolded my precious, yellow possession, as if a new world was opening before my eyes. There it lay in front of me, all deflated, but full of adventurous potential. I ran for a pump and began the laborious, but exciting, task of inflating this new prize. Thirty minutes later I had it up and looking fine. I examined it with great pride. And then, during that moment of silent awe, I heard a noise. It was a constant hissing sound that filled my heart with sadness. I poked at the sides of the raft and could tell that it was softening.

I'll find the hole and patch it. No problem. I asked Dad for some patches. He had some—the good vulcanizing kind. I liked them best, because the rubber would melt securely into place when heated. After the patch was attached, I again pumped up my river-going craft. For a moment, beautiful silence. Then I heard the hissing sound again.

I looked over the yellow raft and found not one, but five more spots that needed patching. I patched them all and inflated my raft once more. And once again, I heard that irritating hissing noise.

Dad was out of patches, so he took me to the store where I bought twelve more. I was now armed and ready for the hissing raft. Needless to say, I found places to put all twelve patches—a total of eighteen holes patched.

I suspiciously and anxiously pumped up the raft for the third time. I heard that same rotten sound. It was as if I had never even slowed the leaks.

I was determined to try it anyway. I was, after all, familiar with leaky boats. I took the raft and the pump and headed to the river. All I can say is it was fun while it lasted, which wasn't very long. I was basically a "floating pumper". After a two-hour workout, I gave up on the raft.

I was furious that someone had the nerve to sell me a piece of junk. I told my sister to get my money back—all six dollars. I don't need to mention the money I lost on the deal. My sister came through for me, though. With the money in pocket, I handed over the yellow raft with blue polka dots, but I didn't give up the search for adventure on water.

BYRON'S JOURNEY

From the Mississippi River
to the Gulf of Mexico
Byron and his kayak
have a long, long way to go.

He leaves behind his wife
and child who he holds so dear.
But they know that he'll be back
before the coming year.

We wish him luck; we wish him well
his journey safe and sound
Byron and his kayak
will soon be homeward bound.

Sally Zastrow 8/17/01

Minnesota
Saint Paul
Wisconsin
Prescott
Madison
Iowa
Des Moines
Illinois
Springfield
Missouri
Jefferson City
Frankfort
Kentucky
Mississippi River
Nashville
Tennessee
Arkansas
Little Rock
Mississippi
Louisiana
Jackson
Atchafalaya River
Baton Rouge
Morgan City

INTRODUCTION

The few days prior to my departure on my Mississippi River journey are busy, yet exciting. Lists are compiled. Supplies are collected. Then comes the task of checking and re-checking my equipment to see if it is necessary for the trip and in good working order. I load the dry bags into my kayak several times to memorize where my equipment will be located. I want retrieval to be quick and efficient in times when it will be critical, such as during times of fog, darkness or inclement weather. Much preparation is necessary for the success of an expedition of this magnitude.

I am asked many times, "Why a kayak?" For me, a sea kayak is the perfect craft for this journey. My boat is 16 feet, 10 inches long, and 23 ¼ inches wide. Three bulkheads divide the kayak into waterproof compartments. It also has a skeg (a ten-inch long fin deployed from a compartment in the rear underside of the hull) to aid in keeping the kayak moving straight ahead in windy conditions. It is a fast and efficient craft that can take waves and cruise through the pools (big, open stretches of water upstream from locks and dams). A kayak has less surface area than a canoe for the wind to catch and force back and forth off course; and ample amounts of necessary gear can be carried in sealed, weatherproof hatches. Besides, I just like paddling a kayak. For me, a solo paddler, it just feels right.

Many friends from my community wish me well with words of encouragement, cards, poems and parties. I am privileged to have my mother, Mary, my sister Cathi and her husband, Jerry, come from Wyoming to help in my preparations and to see me off. The support and help of family and friends are much appreciated.

Bluffs to Bayous

Day 1:

N. 44° 44' 42"
W. 92° 47' 57"

The day of my departure arrives. I lay awake in the early hours of September 4, 2001—not in fear or nervousness, but mostly in wonder. So many questions flash across my mind. *What will it be like to camp in the elements for many days? How long will it really take me? Do I have all the gear I will need? Will I be able to physically paddle day after day?* The questions go on and on. However, this is part of the excitement—the not knowing. Soon, I will have all these questions answered as each day unfolds into an incredible quest.

I rise at 5:00 a.m. *This is it. I may as well get started.* It isn't long before everyone in the house is up, as well. Isaac, my son, helps me load the last few bags into the truck; my kayak and the rest of my supplies were loaded the night before. The truck is ready to go the half-mile to the launch site.

After breakfast, I share a few last moments with Wendi and Isaac. I also have private words with my mom, sister and brother-in-law. I am relieved to get the emotional stuff over with in private.

Within two minutes of our departure at 7:00 a.m., we are at the river's edge. We unload the shiny red and white Current Design Gulfstream kayak and place it gently on the dock. I pack everything in it carefully and deliberately, as every item has a specific place in a dry bag, and every dry bag has a specific place in the kayak.

As I finish strategically placing the final item into the kayak, several well-wishers arrive for my send off. About thirty or so family members and friends are present. I try to thank each one personally with words expressing my appreciation and with hugs or handshakes. I feel privileged to see so many people at my departure.

With Isaac at the bow and I at the stern, we lift the heavy-laden vessel into the water. The audience looks on as I slip into the seat that will be my cockpit for many weeks to come. Isaac and Wendi kneel down on the dock to receive my final good-byes. Isaac then gives me a gentle push away from the dock.

Trying not to sound like a politician, I address the group that has so graciously skipped work to witness my departure. It is incredible to look into their faces, some with glassy eyes, some with excited expressions that seem to say, "I wish I was going," and others look as though they may never see me again. *I need to get away*. With a tip of my hat, I maneuver my kayak away from the dock.

My first strokes are strong and fast. "Pace yourself, Byron!" comes a call from the dock. "You have a long way to go!" I don't look back. The adrenaline pumps furiously through my body, giving way to a smooth, yet powerful, forward touring stroke. The adventure of a lifetime has begun.

It is a radiant September morning. The glowing sun illuminates the wispy fog that covers parts of the river. The air is still, and the pillars of vapor seem to be gently reaching to the sky. I silently thank God for the perfectly beautiful day He has given me to begin my journey.

I paddle for only an hour when I have the urge to pee. *I don't want to have to get out of my kayak already; I'm just getting started. I will use the bottle I brought along for just such an occasion.*

Unsnapping the spray skirt (a covering to keep water out of the cockpit), I position the bottle and begin my duty while slowly drifting with the river's current. Just as I'm half-relieved, a large boat speeds around a curve in the river. I have to decide quickly what to do in this vulnerable situation. *Do I finish my duty or try to stop mid-stream?*

I see that the boat's wake is large and rapidly heading my way. Its waves will hit me broadside. This means the water will splash into the cockpit and get me and the inside of the kayak wet, not to mention spilling the contents of the bottle. *I'm only a few miles into my 1,700-mile journey and not ready to get wet—not just yet.*

Now it takes two hands to put a spray skirt on. *What am I going to do about the uncapped bottle of pee? I don't want the bottle tipping over in the kayak. I better decide quickly, because the swells are pushing me close to shore. I could get gallons of water spilled into my lap if I don't act now!*

A kayaker's view in the lock chamber.

I quickly empty the bottle overboard and throw it into the cockpit. With two hands, I snap the spray skirt into place just as the third wave, eager to soak me, washes over my kayak. *I make it just in time! I hate to dump pee into the water, as it just doesn't seem right. Who knows, I might meet up with it days later downriver!*

With that small ordeal dealt with, I approach the lock and dam near Red Wing, Minnesota—my first of many. I radio ahead to the lockmaster, as they are called, on my waterproof, marine VHF radio. I say, "Lock and Dam 3, this is Kayaker seeking southbound passage."

The lockmaster responds, "It will be fifteen minutes before we can get you through."

I float patiently at the end of a cement wall (several hundred feet long) waiting for the signal to proceed. When the water in the lock has risen to the same level as the river upstream, two huge metal doors swing out slowly. When the doors are fully open, a traffic signal, located near the gate, changes from red to green, giving me the signal to enter. I paddle into the lock and over to the wall. A lock worker throws one end of a rope for me to hold (the other end is securely fastened to the wall). After the upstream doors close behind me, encasing me in four walls with the sky as the ceiling, water is pumped out of the lock. It is incredible to think that all this power and technology is unleashed just for me in my little kayak. When the water level in the lock decreases to the same level as the river downstream, the downstream doors swing open. I must wait for a horn blast before paddling out of the lock and continuing on my way.

After passing through the lock, I make my first stop for lunch. Even though the sun's rays are unobstructed, extreme loneliness comes over me like a dark, heavy cloud. This is my first realization that I am alone and will be for many days to come.

One of my best friends in life gave me some advice, "When you're by yourself, you need to be alert at all times." These are powerful words for a person attempting a solo expedition. If I find myself in a dangerous situation, because I am alone, it could mean life or death. For me, this means no careless drifting in the kayak; no taking unnecessary chances; no wasting my resources; and not using my knife unless absolutely necessary, for a careless cut could end my trip. *I am going to take Mick's advice with me all the way to the Gulf. I cannot allow myself to be overcome with loneliness; I will need to keep focused if I am to complete the task I have set out to accomplish.*

Several pelicans fly overhead. Huge white wings effortlessly propel them south. Life is easy for these masters of gliding—or so it seems. *I wonder if I will meet up with them farther down the river?*

It is about 2:30 in the afternoon when I reach the north end of Lake Pepin, twenty-five miles from my starting point. Normally, I will not stop this early, but to find another campsite, I would have to paddle a long way. *I don't want to push myself too hard the first day. Besides, I will need strength and endurance to paddle the entire length of Lake Pepin tomorrow.*

I study my river maps. I choose the last island before entering Lake Pepin, a long, low island, thickly wooded with river willows. This island will give me a clear view of Lake Pepin. As I paddle around the island, I notice a small sandy shore on its southeast bank. Approaching it, I notice a small opening in the willow trees about thirty feet from the water's edge—the perfect spot for my first campsite.

Paddling twenty-five miles is a respectable distance for the first day. Endurance training and perfecting my paddling skills has kept the aches and pains at bay—at least for today. I am encouraged by my performance, but at the same time, bothered by a nagging nervousness; I still have so many miles to go and so many unanswered questions. I will have to take one day at a time.

With day one behind me, now I must focus on day two. Even though tomorrow's objective is to paddle the length of Lake Pepin, twenty-three miles (two miles less than today's goal), I will face more challenging obstacles. Lake Pepin has no current whatsoever, to aid in my progress. What's worse, if there is a southerly wind, that alone will cause me to strain for each mile, foot, even inch. The waves a wind creates will only add to my struggle. *I hope the winds are as calm tomorrow as they were today. Cooler temperatures would be pleasant, also. Today's high temperature was over eighty, too hot for my liking.*

I anticipated meeting many barges each day since this is the harvest season. Interestingly enough, I didn't see one barge today—a pleasant surprise.

Day 2

N. 44° 33' 34"

W. 92° 25' 37"

I wake at 5:30 a.m., ready to face my first open-water challenge of this trip. Even though I live near Lake Pepin, I haven't had the chance to paddle this pool. The bluffs and trees are silhouetted against the morning sky. The sun will be greeting me shortly with its warm rays. From past paddling experiences, I know that as the sun rises and warms the cool air, the intensity of the wind increases, as well. If I plan to conquer Lake Pepin successfully, I had better get an early start.

After a refreshing night's rest, my body is eager to be paddling again. At 6:15 a.m. I inch my burdened kayak into the glassy water. As I fall into a comfortable rhythm, my red and white Gulfstream slices undauntedly through the placid waters.

The first fifteen minutes of paddling are pure bliss. Then the wind comes knocking ever so gently. However, by the time another hour passes, the beastly wind forces me to hug the shoreline, searching for a reprieve.

Because the wind is from the southeast, maybe I will find relief by crossing over to the Wisconsin side. However, I am concerned about the whitecaps in the middle of the lake. If paddling near shore is a struggle, battling the waves will, no doubt, be treacherous.

I look at the map and choose the shortest distance, about a quarter- to a half-mile across. I check for barges and once again contemplate the situation I am facing. Reminding myself to stay alert and relaxed (tense muscles and a rigid posture can cause kayaks to capsize easily), I charge into the frothy, windswept waters.

Leaning into the wind, I press forward with persistent, steady stokes. I approach the halfway point in good order. Although the waves are only three feet high, there is no time to slack off. I must continue on, for I am more unprotected in the middle of the lake.

Within thirty minutes, I reach the eastern shore. The strength of the wind doesn't weaken. I have to stay within ten feet of land to get the slightest windbreak.

I reach Stockholm, Wisconsin, at lunchtime. A small campground and park border the shoreline. I make a quick stop for lunch and to top off my water supply before tackling the final leg of Lake Pepin.

Despite the wind, I reach the south end of Lake Pepin by 1:30 p.m. As the air temperature increases to eighty degrees, beads of sweat form on my forehead. My arms ache from hours of non-stop paddling. I land at the first favorable beach for a well-deserved break, where for the first time, I can see four to five feet below the water's surface. This will be a convenient time to cool off and a suitable place to clean up.

As I finish washing, a middle-aged man motors up in a small raft.

"Mind if we share this beach?" he inquires.

"Come on in," I welcome.

Wearing only swim trunks, the curly-headed man hops out of his raft. We both find a spot—a hundred yards or so apart—he in the sun, I in the shade.

After resting my sore muscles for an hour, I become restless. I get ready to push off and head for the confluence of the Chippewa and Mississippi rivers, where I anticipate finding an inviting, sandy site to camp for the night.

As I climb into my cockpit, the man from the raft makes his way toward me. "Would you like a soda?" he asks. "I know you don't have much room in those kayaks." As I accept his offer, he asks, "You know about wing dams, don't you?"

"Sure do," I reply as I ease into my kayak.

"You'll be okay then." Gazing in all directions, he adds, "You know this might be the most beautiful area of the whole river!"

I will soon see for myself, I think. *I must say it is very beautiful around here with the sandy beaches, clearer waters and eagles dancing overhead near noble, river bluffs.* This area hosts a high concentration of eagles. *I wonder if the clearer water, making for better visibility, has anything to do with it? Or maybe, they too, think it's the most beautiful place.* The raft man wishes me luck as I paddle toward the main channel.

Shortly, I come to a gently sloping beach sprinkled with shady, maple trees still in their summer's prime. The sugary sand nestles at the bases of the stout river maples just as though it had been deliberately placed there by the high waters of spring. The site offers protection from a northwest wind, yet allows the relaxing, late afternoon sunlight to penetrate the canopy of maples. This will be my campsite at the mouth of the Chippewa River.

In preparation for this trip, I had strategically placed reflective tape on the sides of my kayak. Even though I tie it securely, I check on my boat a time or two during the night by shining my headlight on it. If I am able to see the reflective tape, I can sleep better knowing my kayak is resting safely. My trip will be terminated if strong winds blow my kayak away or if significant fluctuations in the water level float it away in the night.

The nighttime forecast calls for fair weather, so I leave the rain fly off my tent for the second time now. The warm, September breeze gently caresses my tiny shelter. The fresh air induces a much-needed sleep.

Day 3

N. 44° 24' 39"
W. 92° 05' 10"

I depart my campsite this morning at 6:20 a.m. The river runs smooth and quiet, affording me peaceful paddling for the first hour. The soothing calls of water birds add to the serenity. Soon ominous clouds overtake the morning sky, and the weather digresses quickly from tranquil to sodden; I prepare for the first rainfall of my trip.

As I approach Lock and Dam 4, next to Alma, Wisconsin, the river traffic looks clear—no barges. Using my radio, I call the lock. An operator informs me that a barge is about to lock through and the wait will be an hour and a half. I decide against portaging, to avoid possible injury to my boat and myself.

Previous to my departure, I resolved to keep busy while waiting to lock through; by eating, organizing my packs, drying wet gear, etc. I also determined to cook only once a day on my trip. Cooking takes precious time away from more important duties.

I land on a small island about a quarter mile from the lock. The rain subsides, so I choose to prepare my one hot meal; the rest of today's meals will be eaten cold. While cooking rice, I savor the Milky Way candy bar given to me as a farewell gift by Mary Ann, a former coworker. It is one of the best tasting candy bars I have ever had. Just as I finish my rice, it begins to sprinkle.

Thirty minutes into my wait, the barge shows up from behind me. *Surely I could have locked through before the barge had arrived.* The ninety-minute wait turns into a three-hour hold-up. *I could have been six to eight miles down river by now. I remind myself that tomorrow evening I will rendezvous with Wendi and Isaac in Winona, Minnesota, less than a day's paddle away. It is probably better that I have to wait—waiting develops patience.*

After passing through the lock, I continue stroking, enjoying the peacefulness of a quiet river environment. Not many like to travel the river on rainy days, but a group of elderly people was overlooking the river from a high bank in the town of Wabasha, Minnesota.

With hands cupped around his mouth, one calls out, "How far are you going?"

"To the Gulf," I yell back. I keep my pace as they wave and wish me luck.

I pass an A-frame cabin nestled along the shoreline—simple and practical—something Wendi and I would like.

Sometimes I feel strong when I paddle, as if I can go on and on without stopping. I was concerned about developing tendonitis in my wrists, but concentrating on using proper paddling techniques has kept them pain-free, so far. My shoulders ache a little and all my upper body muscles feel well used.

When people ask me, "Doesn't your back hurt with your legs out like that for so long?" I tell them that many hours of sitting in a kayak conditions my body.

For four hours this afternoon it rains, with several heavy downpours. All my stowed equipment is dry and so am I, as long as I wear rain gear and stay in the kayak. I am familiar with camping in the rain, and even though it's not my favorite, I must learn to deal with it and maybe even enjoy it. After all, it is only day three of my trip and undoubtedly, I will have several more days of rain to deal with.

My VHF marine radio has a dual purpose. With it, I can communicate with lock facilities and marine vessels, especially the enormous barges that can't always see a small kayak. It also provides weather forecasts vital to my safety. The NOAA (National Oceanic Atmospheric Administration) weather radio station is predicting more cooler, wet weather. *Looks like tonight I will have the tent fly intact.* The rain is not as miserable as the wind; though, I wish it would change directions. So far the wind has always been against me—in my face. When living out in the elements, I have to be mentally prepared for the weather's harsh conditions.

For camp, I choose the sandy shore of an island near Minneiska, Minnesota. The basketball court-sized island is situated next to the main towboat channel. Several times in the night large barges pass by slowly. The reflections of their running lights on the water's surface have the appearance of Christmas lights. The fronts of barges are quiet; the tows that power them push from the rear. The might of these vessels can never be toyed with. Their slow movements are deceiving shadows of the incredible power that is available with a moment's notice. I watch entire barges pass, and wonder what life is like aboard such a vessel? I drift off to sleep with the muffled drone of a tow making its way up the river.

Day 4

N. 44° 11' 30"
W. 91° 51' 39"

My ritual of early rising continues. I am becoming more efficient at tearing down camp swiftly. Swallowing a couple handfuls of trail mix and a few dried apricots, I'm off by 6:15 a.m. During the night it finally stopped raining, but the wind is already blowing at a pretty good clip. I hug the shoreline; it is a good friend offering me protection from the wind as a token of appreciation for passing by its side.

Tiny, silvery fish, in schools of ten to fifteen, launch themselves into the air each time my paddle touches the water. I'm not sure if they are being playful or inquisitive, or if they are frightened by my paddle chasing them from their watery home. Whatever the reason, I am enjoying the companionship of these small fish.

Because I am quite ahead of my scheduled rendezvous time with Wendi and Isaac in Winona, I decide to stop at the next town, Fountain City, Wisconsin. I pick up my binoculars to scout for a boat launch. An approachable landing awaits me. In my investigation, I spot a Kwik Trip. *I think I will take a little walk to the convenience store.*

Shortly, my kayak is resting on the shore. As I exit to tie up my boat, I notice a sign welcoming visitors to Fountain City. It also contains a street map locating various businesses. As I walk toward town, I pass under a small, arched bridge, which houses the train tracks. I pass a tiny Ford dealership, as I make my way to the Kwik Trip on the main street.

I enter the store and am greeted by a lady cashier of Asian descent and with a southern drawl. "Good morning, y'all."

I look around for the others—no one but me. *I can't possibly be gaining weight!*

The lady must have noticed my confused look. "That's what we say in Texas. I lived there for a long time."

With my best Wisconsin accent, I return the greeting, "Good morning."

She is quite talkative and chipper for the early morn. We have a brief period of superficial chitchat until more customers filter into the store. They too get the same greeting. "Morning y'all."

Even though I don't need any supplies, to be polite, I decide to buy a little something. *Milk, that's what I'm craving.* With a quart of milk and a candy bar in hand, I approach the counter to pay. I must look like I came from the river because the man standing in front of me comments, "I feel sorry for anyone going out on the river today with the bad rains and storm coming."

I leave with my purchases, enjoying the short walk back to the river. Sitting peacefully in the bluffs with its spire churches tucked into the background and its inviting road leading from the dock, this town has a good feeling about it. I savor the last of my milk and candy bar before returning to the cockpit of the Gulfstream. As quietly as I appeared, I leave.

The sky is cloudier and within minutes it begins to rain. I recall the comment of the man at the checkout. *I can handle the rain; it's the lightning I'm leery of.* I shoot back across the river and stay fairly close to the east shore for easy access to its protection.

I arrive at Lock and Dam 5A and head over to the spillway on the west bank. I am to meet Wendi and Isaac nearby.

We are going to camp here together and I'm looking forward to seeing them very much.

It is only 11:15 a.m.; I have a long wait—about five hours. I decide to portage all my gear to a pavilion shelter about 200 yards from the spillway. It takes me an hour to make three trips. On my first trip, I slung several dry bags on each end of the paddle, which I then carried across my shoulders like a stick holding two buckets of well water. I finished carrying the rest of my gear on trip two, leaving my kayak for the final leg. This monotonous transfer confirmed my conviction that doing the least amount of portaging is best.

While under the pavilion, I spread out my wet gear to dry, and I organize the rest. I even have time to nap a little.

Later, as I journal, a Chevy truck pulls up. Two fellows in their late twenties hop out and walk my way. Their baseball caps shade their curious faces. DJ (Dennis) and Derrick are locals of Winona, Minnesota. When they spotted my boat, they wondered what I was up to, since they don't see kayaks very often. After quizzing me about where I was going, what I ate, and the gear I carried, we spend the next two hours jawing about hunting and fishing. I discover that Derrick is one of only a handful of people who has a certain rare disease. Only half of these people ever live and he is one of them. Wow! This is only the beginning of the journey, and I hope to meet many more interesting people during my river quest.

Rain continues on into the afternoon. I am glad to have the pavilion for shelter. After DJ and Derrick leave, I wait patiently for Wendi and Isaac to show. I am very surprised to see them drive up at 4:00 p.m., as I did not expect them for another two hours. We hug and catch up on the latest happenings. Wendi brought emails from friends and family who are concerned for me on the river. She is right in thinking the messages will be an encouragement to me.

While Wendi prepares one of my favorite suppers—fried potatoes and BLT's—Isaac fills me in on the details of his seventh grade football practices and games. He describes some of the exciting, disappointing and sidesplitting plays. I regret not being there to share in these impressionable moments.

The rain continues and the evening goes by quickly—too quickly. The three of us sit cozy in our tent, talking; there is so much to share and so little time. We hope the excitement of being together will help us forget that tomorrow we will again be separated for a long time.

Day 5

N. 44° 04' 46"
W. 91° 40' 58"

By 8:30 a.m. I load everything back into the kayak and am ready to start. It is much harder to say, "Good bye," this time. Four days prior, I knew I would be seeing Wendi and Isaac here in Winona. Now, it will be many weeks before I see them again. I enter my kayak and push off. I linger near shore. It's difficult to leave, but I know I must. I place my paddle in the calm, cool waters and paddle away. Tears well up in my eyes, and I imagine in theirs as well. I look back and wave. They are still watching, and sadly waving. It is a great feeling to know I have two people who love me with unconditional love. Even though each stroke of my paddle takes me farther from them, the bonds of our love and commitment for each other as husband and wife, and father and son, are cemented in my heart and mind.

I secretly hope to see them as they cross the bridge from Winona to Wisconsin. Twenty minutes later, as I am approaching the bridge. I see two people standing on the bank. *It is Wendi and Isaac!* I paddle over and say, "Good-bye," one last time. I hug and kiss Wendi again and start to paddle away.

Wait, I didn't get to touch Isaac! I immediately turn around and paddle back. As I get near the shore, I can see that Isaac's eyes are as watery as mine. We lean to give each other a long, firm hug. We say we love each other, which makes me feel better. I start off again and watch our white truck cross the bridge. They pull over one last time to wave, as we both leave Winona. I wipe the remaining tears from my eyes. *Here I am again, alone on the river.*

Beyond Winona, two large houseboats are resting on my side of the river. Slowly, I maneuver over to say, "Hi." Eight to ten people gather, looking my way.

"What are you doing?" one guy asks.

"Paddling to the Gulf," I reply.

"No way! Are you kidding?"

The conversation is friendly.

Later, another questions, "What do you carry in that thing?"

"Well, just about everything you can imagine," is my answer.

"Do you have a VCR?"

"Well, no."

"The first thing I mention and you don't have one," he jests in good humor.

"I'll be sure to pick one up in the next town," is my jovial response.

By this time, more vacationers, all guys, from Chicago, gather on the decks.

"Do you need anything?" offers one.

"Well, not really."

"How about some soda?"

"Sure, that would be great." There is nothing within reach to steady myself, so I inch as close as I can without bumping into one of the half-beached, half-floating house boats. With a lengthy stretch, a man hands me two Coca-Colas, one at a time. When it's humid and sticky, a cold drink is satisfying.

The group wishes me luck, and with a wave I paddle on, wondering if they pondered my trip for a while after I left, or if they forgot about me as quickly as I disappeared.

There are quite a few fishermen on the river today. I wave or say, "Hi," to everyone I can. Most fishermen are too busy fishing to pay much mind to me, but they are always friendly—not that I need their special attention or anyone else's. I'm not doing this trip for special attention.

Today I passed through Locks 6 and 7 and covered thirty-one miles. Beyond La Crosse, Wisconsin, I find another beautiful island with a sandy shore to beach my kayak and set up camp. After supper, which consisted of rice (flavored with chicken bullion), a bagel, and for dessert, two fun-size Snickers bars, I decide to explore the island. I wear long pants while walking in the grasses and woods. Natural dangers, such as poison ivy and ticks, could cause me misery and suffering on the trip. I also walk the sandy beach in front of my campsite to exercise my legs. Tonight my beach is 151 steps long—a good-sized area.

As I sit on the edge of my kayak, I take a moment to look at my maps and journal about today's experiences.

> *Spending six and a half hours in the kayak today, without getting out, is a good test for me. From talking with others who have traveled the river, I will find more private land and less accessible, public land bordering the Mississippi and Atchafalaya Rivers. Also, landings that cater to small boats will diminish, giving way to hazardously rocky shorelines. Not only this, but obstacles, such as parked barges, may keep me in my kayak for many hours at a time.*
>
> *I also paddle for long periods of time, because I just love to paddle. It helps that the kayak seat is comfortable, too. I'll have to thank Current Designs for that someday.*

About five minutes into thought, I notice another huge houseboat. It turns and heads for my beach. *Looks like I'm going to have visitors.*

The captain nudges the bow of the boat onto the sand, forty yards up the beach from me. One young guy jumps off the boat to set the anchor. Before climbing back on board, he comes over to chat with me. He asks me what I'm doing. By this time I have a pat answer about my trip down the river to the Gulf.

"Wow! You should be on that 'Survivor' show. Have you ever heard of it?"

Did I look like I've been on this river all my life?

"I've heard of it," I answer.

"Come on over, if you want, later."

"Maybe I will."

Just as he returns to the houseboat, the music begins—some type of Rap-flavored music—much too loud for me. I return to my journal, trying to block the music from my mind. Shortly, I glimpse a paddleboat coming up the river. It's playing river tunes. *Boy, that mixed with Rap produces a twisted mix that hardly seems right for this riverside setting.* The paddleboat, Julia Swain, continues upstream in its old-fashioned way on a beautiful sunset evening in September. I decide to pass on the offer to visit the houseboat tonight.

With temperatures dropping into the fifties, I decide to retreat to the warmth of my tent. As I'm lying in my sleeping bag, I reminisce about the time I spent with Wendi and Isaac last night and this morning. These priceless thoughts are with me as I drift off to sleep.

Day 6

N. 43° 46' 15"
W. 91° 14' 48"

I start early, as usual. The weather is still soggy. I never cared for packing away a wet tent. There are some advantages, though, to paddling in damp and misty conditions. The layered clouds and foggy patches that come and go enhance the peaceful and quiet scenery. Also, my body doesn't overheat while paddling and I don't need to wear sunscreen or sunglasses.

During the journey today, I plan to stop in a small Wisconsin town, because a friend of mine knows some people there. She suggested that I stop; she said I could ask for anything I needed. I'm not in need of anything, but I will at least stop to say, "Hello."

As I approach the town, I scan the shores with my binoculars for a landing place, as I usually do. The wind had previously come from the west, so the water, about 30 feet out from shore, is covered with duckweed (tiny, bright yellow-green balls). And just like Styrofoam, this stuff gets on everything. Because the riprap banks make it very difficult to land close to where I need to be and there is no boat traffic to speak of, I tie my kayak to some willows and let it float among the duckweed.

I make my way up the rocky bank, over the railroad tracks, through forty yards of brush and weeds until I finally reach the road. I am farther away from my kayak than I care to be. I did not expect the business to be so far from the river. I will keep the visit brief so I can get back to my unattended kayak quickly.

Approaching the business, all is quiet on the outside. Once inside the workers seem to ignore me. I tell them who I am and what I am doing. They act as though I have interrupted their day, and they could care less about my trip and me. Needless to say, I spend only a brief minute there and head back to the river, slightly disappointed. I didn't expect them to be impressed with me or with what I am doing, necessarily, but just to be friendly, I guess. When I reach the riverbank, my little kayak seems just as eager to get going as I am.

It isn't far to Lock and Dam 8, which I pass through quickly with no difficulties. Beyond the lock, several fishermen in their fancy bass boats with high-powered engines dot the river. They pass me back and forth, sometimes three or four times. As I approach one of the boats, I notice the fishermen aboard seem to be in a hurry, casting all sorts of ways—underhand, overhead and sideways. In a brief conversation, I discover they are professionals competing in a weekend bass tournament.

I have a good paddling rhythm going today—very fast, continuous strokes. As I pass another boat, a bass fisherman yells, "Hey, there's a fifty-five mile per hour speed limit here, you know!"

"Okay," I chuckle, "I'll try toning it down a bit."

A little town on the Wisconsin side is appropriately named Victory. I have just passed my first goal marker—the Minnesota border. I will pass by ten states on my journey—one down, nine to go!

Using the mile markers posted along the riverbanks, I calculate that I have completed thirty-one miles so far today. I begin looking for a campsite. I look down at my map, housed in a waterproof cover, which I keep handy on the deck in front of me. It shows that soon I will happen upon several islands. *Ah, I'll have my choice of camping spots this evening—wrong!* Every single island is either swampy or full of brush and trees, so much so, that I can't even find a place to land. *What happened to all those sandbar islands I had the previous five days?* I can't find a place at all. There is nothing to do, but continue to paddle. However, the water in this particular area is extremely muddy and weedy. It's impossible to make good clean strokes without getting weeds wrapped around the paddle. The farther I go, the more frustrated and exhausted I become. I pause to drink some water and eat a power bar, preparing, as I may have to go as far as the next lock and dam, about fifteen miles away.

More than three hours later, I spot a small island—about two hundred yards before Lock and Dam 9. It's my last hope. After paddling at least 45,000 strokes, my muscles and back are aching now; I need to stop.

The tiny island has a small six-foot long area of sand, a spot just big enough for my tent, with no room to spare. I land and stretch my legs. I turn on the radio to check the weather forecast; NOAA calls for good weather. *Maybe I can get the tent dried out and I won't even need to put the rain fly on.* I set up the tent and spread out my wet things to dry. My muscles are really hurting, so I take some ibuprofen for the first time of the trip. This is my poorest campsite, so far, but I am glad to be resting in my tent. I take a thirty-minute power-nap before preparing rice for supper. I decide to also have a packet of tuna—an extra treat. There's nothing better than food and rest to energize the body. This is my longest day thus far—forty-five and a half miles.

As soon as I finish supper and clean up the dishes, it begins to rain—again. So I hurry around, trying to attach the rain fly. *I thought it wasn't supposed to rain?* Tomorrow I hope for a sunny, sandy campsite to get all dried out. The simple pleasures of life, like a dry shelter, seem so wonderful at times like these.

About 8:00 p.m. a beaver swims back and forth along the shoreline. He slaps his tail on the water several times during the night. *I don't think he likes me being here. Too bad, I'm not moving!*

Day 7

N. 43° 12' 56"
W. 91° 06' 06"

At this point, I have developed a small list of ailments. Because I have a sore above each Achilles heel, I decide to pack away the neoprene boots and wear the water shoes I brought along. Each day, I have been paddling the first four hours barehanded, in an attempt to toughen up my hands. I then wear leather baseball gloves for the rest of the day. Nevertheless, three blisters appear on the palm of my right hand just below the fingers and one appears on my left hand. To ease the discomfort while paddling, I let the paddle rest on my lower palms, relaxing the fingers. I am not sure what to do about a very sore right shoulder, though.

My body needs rest, so I try sleeping in this morning. Despite restless sleep and the aches and pains, I'm up at 6:45 a.m.; I can't stay in my tent any longer. To me, I'm wasting time. If I'm not paddling, I'm not going down the river.

Because my camp is close to the dam, I hope to lock through quickly and be on my way before traffic gets heavy. *Well, no such luck!* The lockmaster is putting a tow through from the south and it will be about an hour's wait.

I tie up my kayak at the end of the long wall and decide to spend my sixty minutes utilizing the lock facilities. From the pay phone, I call my wife at work; it's always good to hear her voice. I pass on to her my GPS coordinates that I take at every campsite, which she will pass on to a Prescott High School teacher who uses them in his math class to determine my mileage for the day. Also, other friends and family are then able to keep track of my progress. More importantly, I keep daily GPS recordings because if something happens to me on the river, my wife can give my last coordinates to aid the people looking for me.

After our quick phone conversation, I go up onto the observation platform, from which, visitors can view the lock process. I find brochures with detailed maps of the pools. These maps are more comprehensive then mine. Since I am in Iowa, and no longer in Minnesota, I had run out of the good maps that the State of Minnesota makes specifically for canoeing in its territory. A lock worker informs me that all future lock and dams have facilities similar to this one. Hereafter, as long as there are lock and dams, I will utilize the phone for calling home, restroom for cleaning up and the fountain for replenishing my water supply.

I am also informed that it will be only ten minutes before I can lock through. I grab a pool map before scrambling back to my waiting kayak. Shortly, the barge leaves and I am signaled to come on through.

After leaving the lock, I notice someone on the west shore. Looking through my binoculars, I see that it is another kayaker, the first one I've seen so far on my trip. Obviously, I would be curious about a fellow kayaker, so I paddle for the Iowa shore.

At his sandy campsite he is about some daily chores when I paddle up. "Hi. How's it going?" I ask.

"Is that you, Curtis?"

I am surprised by his question. "Yes. How did you know?"

"A guy on a barge yelled to *me* yesterday, 'Is that you, Curtis?' I told him I wasn't Curtis, and then he handed me a newspaper article about Byron Curtis kayaking down the river. I read all about you. I'll never be able to keep up with you, though. I can't average thirty miles a day—twenty maybe." Mike, a pipe fitter from the Minneapolis area, has a high-quality kayak crafted in Great Britain, an NDK (Nigel Dennis Kayak) Explorer, painted British racing green. He began his trip in the Twin Cities area, hoping to paddle the Mississippi River to the Gulf, but he's not sure how far he will go.

Curious, I ask him how much water he carries. "Five quarts," he answers. I tell him I don't think that is enough. I carry twelve quarts. Using about three quarts a day, I have enough water for four days, theoretically. I try not to go more than three days without replenishing my water, leaving me with an emergency supply of three quarts. After St. Louis, after the last dam, there will be fewer towns along the river. Also, these river towns are located farther away from the river's banks, making them difficult, even impossible, to reach. This will greatly impact my ability to replenish dwindling supplies. I hope twelve quarts of water will be enough, as the Mississippi River becomes more remote.

In response to my dissertation he says, "I drank the river water once, after boiling it and adding purification tablets. I figure it's at least 90 percent water."

"It's the 10 percent I'm worried about," is my reply.

I wish we could spend more than thirty minutes together, but the river is calling me. Before heading back to the channel, we each snap a couple of pictures and exchange phone numbers.

Three hours later, about noontime, I notice someone else on shore. I again use my binoculars to look the situation over. It's a man in a rowboat with a small motor. He is busy putting a lot of *stuff* into his interesting craft, including a small dog kennel, so it appears.

Wow! This guy is really carrying a lot of gear. Well, to each his own, I guess. At this point I feel very free and mobile, not having to pack and unpack so much *stuff* everyday. We are quite a distance apart and I do not want to stop, so I paddle on by.

About four hours later, I find a campsite at the confluence of the Wisconsin and Mississippi Rivers with a dense woods towering over a narrow, sandy shore. As I'm setting up camp, I look upstream. Here comes the guy in the rowboat, slowly moving down the channel. He stops rowing to fire up his little motor. His boat is loaded so heavy that it doesn't have much free board; most of the boat is below the water's surface. He sluggishly motors by. If he doesn't get too far ahead, maybe I will see him again, tomorrow perhaps.

I chose to stop early today. I paddled only eighteen miles, but wanted to dry out and let my body recuperate from yesterday's arduous paddle. After all, I have a long, long way to go yet, and I don't want to have to quit because of something like tendonitis.

Speaking of drying out, one of my chores each evening, and especially after a sunny day like today, is to wash clothes. I need to do this early on when I first make camp, so the wet clothes have time to dry. Well, today I solved the ring-around-my-T-shirt mystery. Every evening since my journey began, I noticed that the bottom four inches of my T-shirt has been colored purple. *Why is this happening?* For the past week, I have been wearing the same colored underwear (let's get this straight—different underwear, same color). When I tuck my clean, damp shirt into my pants, my underwear dyes a purple ring around the bottom of my T-shirt. Mystery solved. *I wonder what other colors I will find? Maybe I'll have tie-dye T-shirts by the time this trip is over!*

Tonight for supper, I again have rice. This time I add the last of my Wisconsin Colby cheese to it. Delicious!

During the last minutes of light, I sit by the river and am reminded of my dad. I miss the good times we had together in the outdoors. I softly sang some of the old hymns he liked. I'm not a good singer, but I don't think he'd mind.

I retire to my tent and drift off to sleep, listening to the soothing sounds of wildlife. I hear the first coyote howl of the trip. Since my tent is in the woods tonight, I can clearly hear the owls hooting. I think there are four of them, all in different directions. During the night, I awaken to the hoots of owls and the gentle footsteps of a deer wading in the water.

Day 8

N. 42° 59' 18"
W. 91° 09' 19"

September 11, 2001, my birthday. No heavy dew on the tent, so I can put it away dry for a change. Physically, I'm doing better; I only had to take pain pills after the 45.5-mile day. All blisters and joints seem to be healing. It is going to be a great day!

.I start paddling at 6:20 a.m. A thick, soupy fog hangs in the air. For about a half hour I stay within sight of shore, but the fog intensifies, forcing me to within thirty feet. Sometimes I have to cautiously navigate by map. I hear a barge making its way upriver; it is getting closer, but I can't see it. I stay clear of the main channel until it passes. It is an eerie feeling to suddenly see a dinosaur-sized mass appear out of the fog less than fifty yards away. It is two and a half hours before the fog passes.

I feel truly grateful to be on the river today. Not many people get a chance to experience the dream I am fulfilling. Many who are presented with the opportunity, never take the first step to make it happen. A few feel it's a gross waste of time. For me it's an adventure of a lifetime I couldn't pass up. I feel I have made a good choice, and this morning it begins to sink in.

I can feel an increase in the current today compared to when I left home. The river seems a bit wider, too. It is exciting to see changes in the river; it feels like I'm exploring new territory.

Close to 10:00 a.m., I see him again—the man with a rowboat, too much gear and the dog kennel. *He's on the same side of the river as I am…it's time to meet this guy.*

He is breaking camp when I pull up in the kayak. "Good morning," I greet him.

He looks up and comes down to the river's edge. "Are you the writer—the newspaper writer?"

"No, but I was *in* the newspaper, though," I respond.

"Oh, that's right. I heard about you. I was told to look for a red kayak." Mark started his trip on August 20, 2001, from Bloomington, Minnesota. He is headed to the Florida Keys. *Maybe that's why he has so much stuff.* He doesn't have a dog, but a cat. Actually, he started his trip with two cats, but one fell sick and had to be put to sleep in Prairie Du Chien, Wisconsin.

We chat for a while about our trips and gear and *stuff.* After taking pictures of each other, I part. *A very interesting person—I wonder if I'll ever see him again?*

I paddle very hard after that. I don't know why; it just feels right.

Up ahead, I can see that a barge is halfway through Lock and Dam 10. Assuming it won't be a long wait, I decide to take a short break. After using the restroom, I proceed to the observation deck to check on the progress of the barge. Several elderly tourists are video taping the locking process. They ask permission to tape me, as well. I give them a few particulars about my voyage. They give me a few details about some sort of terrorist attack in New York City—something about planes crashing into buildings—it's all so sketchy. As I had calculated, the barge vacates the lock in short order. I quickly return to my kayak, as I am next in line.

Previous to my leaving Prescott, I had set up a Yahoo account on the Internet with the intent to send and receive email

A birthday celebration like no other.

messages from family and friends during my trip. I had communicated by email with a couple during their canoe trip down the Mississippi a year before, and thought it might be a good idea for my journey, as well. I decide to stop in Cassville, Wisconsin, to see if I can find a public library to send email to Wendi. After walking four miles and wasting about two hours, I finally find it; it's closed. The sign on the door gave its hours—closed Sunday and Tuesday. *Of all days for me to pick—a Tuesday.* I decide it's not worth the time and effort to ever do that again; it's better to call home. As long as I'm here, though, I get water at the riverside park before heading back to my kayak.

I paddle hard again until my back muscles begin to ache. Shortly after 3:30 p.m., I locate a small, sandy island. I set up the tent, hang wet clothes to dry, and make supper. *Now, it's time for my birthday treat*! Mom and my sister Cathi gave me a Snickers bar for this very occasion. Steve and Penny, some friends of mine from Prescott, sent along a birthday candle. I drill a hole into the top of the candy bar with my Leatherman tool; insert the candle; and *"Wa-la! Happy Birthday!"* Lighting the candle is difficult, but taking a picture of myself blowing it out before the wind does, that's even more difficult. It tastes delicious. I am now, I feel, officially 39 years old.

After looking at maps for a while, I determine that I have covered 209 miles from my starting point. This is satisfying enough; nevertheless, it is only a short sprint compared to the miles I have yet to cover.

At 6:00 p.m. I sit down to write in my journal. Shortly, I hear a small motor coming down the river. *No, it couldn't be, could it? Yes, It's Mark in his over-loaded rowboat.*

He approaches. "Mind if I share this campsite with you?"

"Come on in." I motion him in with my hand. *Maybe I'll get to know this interesting guy a little better.*

He has a special way he lands his boat, so I don't need to help him. Soloists have to develop techniques like this. We can't always depend on someone being there to help. After situating his boat, he begins the chore of setting up camp.

"Do you want a Coke?" he asks. "Ice?"

"You have ice?" *What <u>doesn't</u> he have?*

"Yeah. I get five pounds every few days for a treat." He hands me a big bag of ice and another bag full of pop. "Help yourself."

Something cold to drink is refreshing after a day in the sun. Mark proceeds to dig out a comfy-looking folding chair and a radio, offering them both to me. *Wow! Maybe he doesn't have too much gear after all.*

He asks me if I have heard the news. "Well," I respond, "some tourists at the last lock and dam made mention of an attack on New York City. I don't know any other details." He turns the radio on and tunes into the world news, listening for updates.

"Two planes crashed into the World Trade Center Towers this morning. Both buildings have since collapsed. It is estimated that several thousand people have lost their lives. A third plane crashed into the Pentagon in Washington D.C., and a fourth crashed in Pennsylvania, never reaching its mark..."

Wow! I'm sorry this happened. Now that the news-caster mentions it, I haven't seen or heard any aircraft flying overhead today. I feel like I've traveled back in time, before technology—before the telephone, radio, television and the

Internet. Here I am, peacefully paddling down the middle of the country, while the entire nation is completely fixated on one tragic event. What a sobering moment in history—and on my birthday.

After Mark is situated, we talk for a couple of hours. Mark is quite the interesting person. He was a U.S. Marine in his time, and for several years he climbed mountains professionally. Four times he scaled the Alaskan Mount McKinley, and he had planned to climb Mount Everest, but it didn't pan out. He said he came close to death so many times that it was time to get out of the mountain climbing business. Mark's goals have changed from climbing to rowing and sailing. He looks a bit peculiar with his jumbled up hair and his lanky thin body, but I guess it just goes to show, you can't judge a man by his hairstyle. It is really nice to have Mark's company tonight.

In case you are wondering, his cat's name is Maestro.

Day 9

N. 42° 41' 02"
W. 90° 55' 16"

I sleep soundly through the night, but am up and ready to go before Mark and Maestro stir. I travel early and stop early, whereas Mark gets up late and travels late; it works well for each of us even though it's different. In the chair he set out for me last night, I leave a note thanking him for the pop and ice, and wish him well on his journey to the Florida Keys. *Maybe we'll meet again sometime, Mark.*

Refreshed from a good night's sleep, I paddle hard all morning, passing an occasional barge or fisherman. I find myself two miles from Lock and Dam 11, when I notice a tow behind me. Knowing that barges have precedence at locks, I will use the extra time to get water at the facilities.

I pull in behind the lock's long wall. Some locks have floats to tie up to, but this one has nothing, just cement and rock. Jagged rocks all around make it very difficult to enter and exit a kayak. Coming up with an alternate plan, I place an old drift log between my kayak and the sharp rocks, like the rubber floats a captain uses between his boat and the dock. I exit carefully and secure my kayak. I approach the lock house, noticing the American flag is flying at half-staff. A worker watches me closely and meets me at the bathroom door.

"Where did you come from?" he questions. "This place is closed to the public. Did you come off a boat?"

"I came from my kayak over there," I respond, pointing behind me and to my right.

"The bathrooms are locked to the public, but I'll let you in since you came off a boat."

"It will take about two hours to get the tow through," the worker adds. "Will you portage instead of waiting?"

"No, I'll just rest until it's my turn."

I lay down on the bench of the picnic table, shaded by a towering oak. I close my eyes for a few minutes. Not wanting to miss my turn through the lock, I lift my head and look around from time to time. The worker is raking leaves scattered on the lock grounds. It seems every time I look up, he stops raking to watch me. Up until this point, I haven't been too concerned about the effects of the terrorist attack on my trip. It seems, though, that passing through locks may become a challenge.

It isn't a half hour before the lock master calls to me, "We'll be ready for you in twenty minutes."

I grab Pool Map 12 before heading back to the river. By the time I situate myself back into the kayak, the lock master motions me into the lock, even though the gates are open only about ten feet. The lock doors begin to close behind me as soon as I pass the opening. I didn't get a rope to hold onto this time. *They must want to get me through quickly.* Shortly, the exit gates open revealing a northbound barge waiting to get in. *I'm surprised they sent me through before this other barge. Maybe my presence makes them nervous. I'm just glad they let me through—period.*

Shortly after passing through Lock and Dam 11, I complete my second state, Wisconsin, and begin the long descent along the Illinois border. On the western bank sits Dubuque, Iowa, my first large river city. Numerous parked barges congest the river. It isn't unusual to come within six feet of these floating masses. I have to keep a sharp eye out and do some fast paddling and fancy maneuvering as tows weave among these cold, steel monsters.

As I pass through the city, the number of parked barges along both shores increases. Sometimes there are as many as thirteen barges parked side by side from the shore out towards the channel. This can be a dangerous predicament for a small boat to be in, as it's hard to tell what's around the barge, or if a tow will suddenly start to move them.

Before I left home, I had paddled among these heavy weights of the river many, many times. Now far from home, I have seen their sizes increase and I am much more careful around them. Sometimes I can hear the dull drone of the diesel engines long before I ever spot the beasts. I always give them plenty of room and the respect they deserve. They seem like huge floating creatures that take no survivors of those who are foolish enough to challenge them. Yet, deep inside are skilled pilots and crews with families and lives like me. I am always impressed with the way they guide these massive cargo carriers down the river. My hats off to them!

I finally get beyond Dubuque, away from the barge congestion, and start my daily task of campsite hunting. Sometimes it's easy to find one, sometimes it's hard. I finally find a spot that looks good from a distance and paddle for it. As I am a hundred yards from landing, a boater in a johnboat pulls up on the shore. Landing next to him, he asks, "Where you headed?"

"To the Gulf."

"I've seen people do that before, but never in a kayak.... Pretty small.... Camping here tonight?"

"Planning on it."

"This place is trashy. I know a better place a couple of miles downriver."

I listen, but one can never be too sure about another's directions. *How far are a couple of miles anyway?* What seems like two miles in a motorboat, may be five miles in a kayak. He points to a spot on my map and is confident that I can find it. He says it has a picnic table and chairs, too. *A place to sit comfortably—that sounds nice*. I decide to trust him and go for it.

Before we part, he warns me about the bad currents and big barges below St. Louis. "I don't want to read about your death in the paper," he adds. I assure John I will be careful.

I paddle a little more than two miles and find the densely wooded island John had described. The landing is a bit cumbersome—the bank is a little high. For my tent, I find an airy location under the trees where the firm sandy ground keeps the weed growth to a minimum. I quickly go about my evening chores of eating supper and organizing my gear, so that I can explore this paradise island.

On the picnic table sits eight Citronella candles. Six to eight white plastic patio chairs are stacked near the table. On the back of each chair is marked "TUNA BEACH". *Interesting, since there's no beach and likely, no tuna.* Two small, narrow tables, scarred by deep gouges, have remains of fish scales. Forty yards to my right, I spy a blue tarp. It is wrapped around an area of trees hiding a pit toilet. Two rolls of toilet paper stay dry in a plastic bag. *John was right. This is a much better location.*

Slivers of the evening sun pierce the shady canopy of large maples announcing the potential arrival of mosquitoes. Choosing the cleanest chair, I face it towards the river. I strategically place the eight candles, some on chairs, some on the ground, in a circle around my chair. I spend the last remaining minutes of daylight recording today's events. Unable to keep my eyes open any longer, I retire to my small tent.

The stout trees towering above seem to quiet the breezes and the river noises, but at the same time, amplify the sounds of the night. Crickets, owls, and unfamiliar creatures serenade me as I sleep.

Day 10

N. 42°25' 11"
W. 90° 33' 10"

I leave in the early dawn—6:20 a.m. to be exact. My arms are feeling stronger each day, so once again, I paddle hard and steady, stopping only for a quick meal, to apply sunscreen or to use the binoculars. I guess I'm not the dilly-dally type. As a matter of fact, I have a difficult time going slow. For me, drifting with the river at about one mile per hour is a waste of time—pure torture.

The brochure I have indicates that there is no public restroom at Lock and Dam 12, so I don't stop for water either. I am fortunate to be able to lock through right away. Some of the workers watch me maneuver my kayak into position as I approach the rope they have for me. One guy comments, "You sure know how to control that thing." I imagine he has seen many intriguing people lock through, in all kinds of floating things.

So far, the wind has been at my back, but by 10:30 a.m., the wind switches directions. To seek relief from its abuse, I am forced to cross to the Illinois side, which poses a problem. Twenty miles of the Illinois bank belongs to the Savanna Army Depot. Several signs warn that this area is off limits to everyone. I can figure that I will be restricted to my kayak for at least four more hours. Normally, twenty miles of non-stop sitting is not a big problem, but I have already been in the kayak for some hours and am in need of a stretch. *I could cross back over to the other side of the river, I suppose, and brave the winds that now have increased to migraine headache strength.* Seeing that two thirds of the river is covered with whitecaps, resembling a lemon meringue pie, I decide to stay with the Savanna Army Depot.

Up ahead I notice several unique buoy markers. Unlike the usual channel and mile markers that have dotted the river this far, they outline a large, half-moon shaped area that is a third of the river's width at the widest point. I approach one of the buoys to read the warning, "DANGER. UNEXPLODED ORDINANCES IN AREA. DO NOT ENTER." I quickly snap a picture with my camera as the current deceptively sucks my kayak into the restricted area. I sprint to the outside of the buoyed area, facing the wind and whitecaps to get around.

Shortly after passing the quarter-mile danger zone, I hear several gunshots. I am reminded of the time when my coworker, Rick, threatened to sink my kayak. He is an ex-military man, himself, and I could picture him leading a group of military sharp shooters to the river's edge and shouting, "There he is! Sink his kayak, but don't hurt him. He's got a lot of work to do back in Prescott." I guess you could say Rick and I had some good times at work.

After about four and a half hours of constant paddling, I pass the Army Depot. My kayak is still floating, but my butt is pretty sore; I have been sitting in the Gulfstream for six and a half hours straight.

Flying from an island up ahead, I see a huge, I mean really big, American flag, about fifteen by thirty feet in size. Six or seven boats are beached beneath it. I maneuvered to within ten feet of a man cleaning fish. "How's it going?" I ask.

The man looks up with a start. "Oh, fine."

"What's going on here?" I question.

"Well, a bunch of us get together every year to have a big camp out."

From the size of the flag I can image how big this camp out must be. "How many people are camping?" I count fifteen tents.

"By tonight, there should be a hundred or more."

Keeping true to my main trip objective, I conduct this conversation from the seat of my kayak, like I have many times previous. Never once, including now, has anyone seemed to be offended when I didn't get out of my kayak to talk. Maybe it's my non-aggressive appearance, or maybe it's my slow-moving, human-powered craft, that puts everyone at ease. My motives are pure; I want to see and do as much as possible from the river, so as to get its perspective.

This man doesn't ask what I am doing or where I am headed, and I don't feel compelled to tell him. I just continue on my way, keeping an eye out for a solitude place to rest my weary body.

Tonight I stop on an island, just short of my goal of thirty miles. According to my map, if I paddle two more miles, I will come upon another town and that might mean more barge traffic and pleasure boaters to deal with. Besides, I'm not fond of dodging barges with a sore, tired back.

Although my back is sore, my shoulders and hands have healed and are not giving me a bit of trouble. *Maybe they have become more hardened and used to the pace I am asking them to keep.* The only thing that seems to bother me lately is my back. Sometimes it's a muscle low in my back or sometimes it's a shoulder blade muscle. Nevertheless, life on the river has been treating me well. I've no major ailment to complain about, except for the loneliness I feel while away from my family.

I place my tent on an intimate opening—the only opening on this five-acre island. For supper, I eat instant potatoes and powdered eggs. Both are delicious, but I cooked the eggs too long. They stick like glue to the sides of the pan, making it difficult for even a mountain man with muscular arms to scrub the pan clean. Since I camp mostly in sandy areas, I use the sand as a scrubbing agent to clean dirty pans. Put a couple handfuls of sand in the pan; add a cup of water *and "Presto! Clean pots!"* Sand can make a pan shine in no time, that is, unless I cook the super glue egg mix!

Tonight is my night to shave. I try to do this every couple of days, so as not to scare the people I come in contact with. Just because I'm on the river, doesn't mean I should look like a stray. It must be amusing to see me squatting while peering into a two-inch, round Precious Moments mirror. Catch your breath and let me explain.

While collecting necessary equipment for my trip, I kept my eye open for a small, lightweight mirror. However, the mirrors I found were either too bulky or too heavy. At my mother-in-law's garage sale, Wendi picked up this little, Precious Moments mirror (not exactly what a river rat would choose, but it's compact and virtually weightless).

I can't see my whole face in it at one time—only parts. I seldom get a glimpse of my whole face. It's probably better this way. You can be sure I am alone when I pull out the mirror.

For the first time on my trip, I light a campfire. I'm not sure why. *Maybe it's easy to get wood here. Maybe I use it to cut through the evening's dampness.* I gaze at the pulsating coals—the television of the solitude. *How truly fortunate I am to be on this peaceful secluded island.*

I write in my journal until I am distracted by the sound of an outboard motor. Looking up, I guess it to be a commercial fisherman's boat because of the large tub he uses to hold his catch. The boat suddenly veers from the channel and approaches my campsite.

Using a ten-foot pole, the captain of the boat gently nudges his craft up onto my beach.

"Where'd you come from?" he asks.

"Wisconsin."

"And how far you going?"

"To the Gulf."

"That's an incredible trip you're taking. What are you going to do after you pass St. Louis? The river is really big down there and the barges are huge." He speaks to me with great knowledge and concern.

"I'll be careful and alert."

"I suppose you'll stay close to the shore." Looking around at the dense vegetation he questions, "Do you know about some of the poisonous plants around here?"

"I know about poison oak (that's what we called poison ivy when I was a kid)."

"There's poison ivy and poison sumac, too. They can make life really miserable for a person."

Curious, I ask him to describe poison sumac. With hip boots rolled down below his knees, he jumps from his boat and leads me into the woods. "It has a woody stalk, something like this plant. This looks like a young one here. Be careful of this stuff. If, by accident, I break out, I put Carmex on it right away. Carmex seems to help keep it from spreading much. Do you have any Carmex?"

I never realized it could be so useful. "I have one tube with me."

We return to the waters edge, catching the last glimpse of the waning sunlight. Gordy works about sixty miles of the river. Briefly he explains the setline process he uses to catch catfish. He also continues to share more of his wealth of river knowledge and warns me again about the river below St. Louis. "It's big!"

As we walk the short distance to Gordy's boat, he adds, "I stopped because I find guys like you interesting to talk with. I read a book once about a guy who came down the river in a canoe, and how he describes some of the little towns along the river that I know of."

"That's all the further they make them for," Gordy says, as he hands me a pool map; I am glad to get it.

In minutes, darkness will be upon us. We shake hands as he wishes me safety on the river. Gordy gives his boat a shove and hops in. After starting his motor, his silhouette disappears down river. I stand motionless for a moment, wondering about Gordy—thankful for his visit. I turn to the fire, its warmth fading.

As I slip into my sleeping bag, the sounds of crickets, frogs and the occasional bird tuck me into bed.

Day 11

N. 42° 07' 45"
W. 90° 11' 48"

A clear, star-filled sky greets me this morning. A chill comes over me at 6:20 a.m., as I stuff the last items into the kayak. I cock my head toward the river. *It's too dark for a boat to be on the water, isn't it? How can he navigate? He must be a fisherman, familiar with every bend and current in the river.*

.The boat motors directly to my campsite. I am excited to see Gordy again before pushing on. "Good morning." I help pull Gordy's boat ashore.

"You have beautiful stars over a crescent moon to paddle under this morning!" he announces. "I came back for a couple reasons." Gordy reaches into his pocket, pulling out a new tube of Carmex. "Here," he says, handing me the gift. "You probably could use this at some point in your trip. It works good for me." He then hands me a paperback book, which he pulls from behind his back. "I thought you might find this interesting." The low light conditions keep me from seeing the title of the book. I take it and thank him. I feel truly blessed that a stranger is willing to stop a second time to give me gifts.

Gordy then says something that I will carry with me the rest of the way down the river. "I want to tell you something about the trip you're taking. Not many people get a chance to do what you're doing, but I wish that I would someday. There are going to come times when you get wet, cold, or when you feel like you've had enough of this old river. You'll feel like quitting; you'll feel like going home. Don't do it!" he exhorted. "Finish the journey you started. Don't give up and don't quit. Just keep going and you'll be glad you did." He repeats, "Don't quit!"

We shake hands one last time and go our separate ways. Still not knowing what it's about, I pack the book in a dry bag before pushing away from the shore. I look down river and there it is, as beautiful as ever, the crescent moon under the stars, just as Gordy had said. I appreciate the words Gordy gave me. What an incredibly encouraging start to this early morning, September 14. I realize that I have well over 1,000 miles yet to go, and I may very well feel like quitting, but I will always remember Gordy's words.

I paddle past sun-up, enjoying the calm conditions, for now. The forecast calls for southeast winds, which will be here soon, along with the jumbled water caused by the day's activities. The wind eventually comes, but mostly from the east. It seems to change at times, following the river's path.

By 10:00 a.m. my back muscles are giving me grief. Normally, I like to keep my life jacket snug so that it won't ride up around my neck in case I capsize. However, I need relief from my back pain, so I loosen the straps on my life jacket to see if this will help. Amazingly, my back instantly feels better. I guess my life jacket is too tight after all, hindering my muscles from flexing with each stroke.

Eager to conquer close to thirty miles, I find myself in a rush. I need to pace myself, as I have a long way to go yet. Although it's difficult, I force myself, on occasion, to stop, get out of the kayak and take a mandatory break.

Pool 13 seems endless. One of the workers from Lock and Dam 11 warned me about this pool. "I used to work at Lock and Dam 13," he says with authority. "The river's four miles wide there and the waves can get real big—seven foot!" he warns. "We've had to rescue people many times....Be very careful!"

It *is* big, just like he said. I try not to get more than a mile from land, in case I need to seek its safety. Fortunately, I have a slight, northeast breeze in my favor. After about four hours of paddling, I am able to pass through Lock and Dam 13 with no problems, glad to be free of this enormous and potentially dangerous pool.

Looking for a place to take a well-deserved lunch break, I come upon a few islands dotting the river near Clinton, Iowa. Rounding one of the islands, I see a man lounging on a sandbar, his powerboat anchored offshore.

I glide the nose of my kayak onto the beach. "Hi. How's it going?"

"Great," he says. "Enjoying the good weather." He flashes me a friendly smile. "I thought you were a friend of mine; he kayaks a lot." The man takes a drink from his can. "Where you from?"

"Wisconsin," I answer. "I'm headed to the Gulf."

"That's a long trip in a kayak."

We talk while I eat trail mix, washing it down with water. John is from Chicago and is taking a year off from work. This is one of his favorite places to hang out, "...so relaxing and calm here at the river." Come to find out, John's a millionaire. *No wonder he can take a year off.* When he was young, he invested in a strong stock market, making big money. He's also a computer software designer; he knows Bill Gates and other big names, personally. *Must be nice, but I'm glad I don't have to be a millionaire to enjoy the river.*

Soon it is time for me to head out again. I slip back into the river's current. The sun shines through puffy white clouds. *It is a beautiful day!*

Instinctively, about mid-afternoon, I begin my search for tonight's campsite. The first few locations I contemplate are either too muddy or too brushy to pitch my tent. *I have a few more miles left in me, and there's got to be something better, so I'll keep looking.* However, the farther I go, the worse the possibilities get. After ninety frustrating minutes, when I am about to settle for a miserable location, I convince myself to look around one more bend. *Wow! An incredible sandbar about 200 yards long, 40 yards wide and all to myself. I'm glad I looked around one more corner.*

I set up my tent and go about my evening chores. I strip down to my underwear and take a quick sponge bath. Because the air is chilly this evening, I immediately put on clean clothes from my dry bag before washing the dirty ones I just took off.

I take off my dirty clothes to rinse them in the Mississippi, removing the sweat and dirt. Often, if the air temperature is moderate to warm and the wind is breezy, I hang them to dry on low branches or on my paddle wedged upright in the sand. Sometimes, as soon as a half hour, I'm able to put my clothes back on. *This seems like a decent system; it works for me.*

The only concern I have about this campsite is that the tent and kayak are separated by fifty yards. I prefer to be closer to my equipment, so I can watch over it better. The greater the distance between kayak and camp, the greater the chance of misplacing critical gear somewhere and leaving it behind. All my gear is essential and to lose any one thing could be detrimental to my success.

After paddling 38.5 miles today, I'm ready for a good night's rest.

Day 12

N. 41° 41' 36"
W. 90° 19' 12"

Even though I dropped off to sleep quickly last night, I had a fitful night's rest. Even though I'm prepared to leave at my usual time, I still feel very tired. I tell myself I will stop earlier tonight to rest up; we'll see.

This morning I look for a phone to call Wendi, which I try to do every three-days or so. If possible, I prefer to "kill two birds with one stone," as they say—stop once for water and a phone. I notice a small town on the map called Port Byron. *Now, that sounds like a friendly place, and indeed it is.* The dock area caters to small vessels and a sign expresses a warm welcome to everyone. I can see that the main street is not far from the river, so I set off in search of a pay phone.

Before I left on my quest, my wife made a small calendar for me, about the size of a large index card. On one side is September 2001 and on the other side, October 2001. Wendi wrote in all the activities that she and Isaac had scheduled, so that I would know when and when not to call home. I know Wendi and Isaac are at a volleyball tournament today, but I want to leave them the message that I am safe and well.

Back on the river, I make my way toward Lock and Dam 14 and the Quad Cities of Davenport and Bettendorf, Iowa, and

Moline and Rock Island, Illinois. Like Lock 13, I pass through Lock 14 very quickly; I don't have to wait for barges. As I paddle past Moline, I notice the John Deere factory. There seems to be a lot of industry in Moline. In Bettendorf I spy a park. *Maybe I can fill up with water.* As I pull up next to this riverside park, I greet a couple of boys, about fourteen years old, on their bikes. "Hi guys. How you doing?"

"Okay." They edge themselves and their bikes out from behind a tree. "Is that true what your kayak says, you're going from 'Wisconsin to the Gulf'?"

"Sure is, guys." I answer the many questions Chris and Scott have for me. They aren't full of preconceived thoughts and attitudes about everything like adults sometimes are. They are like sponges, soaking in life's information.

I ask them if they will watch my kayak while I look for water nearby. They agree enthusiastically.

With full water bottles, I return to Chris and Scott who are full of more questions, which I gladly answer. I also tell them I may write a book about this trip some day and ask permission to put their names in it.

"Well, what will the book be called, so we can read it?" they ask with excitement.

"I'm not sure, yet." I give them my name for an author search.

They watch me slip into my kayak; it's time for me to paddle on. Not wanting me to leave, they ride their bikes along side my floating kayak for a ways. So, Scott and Chris of Bettendorf, Iowa, I hope you read this book someday and see your names in it. It was nice meeting you in September of 2001.

Shortly, I reach Lock and Dam 15. I notice a barge entering the lock, so am puzzled when the lockmaster tells me my wait is only ten minutes. I assumed it would have been at least an hour, as that is roughly the time it takes to get one of these brutes through. A man on a long wall motions for me to come over his way. This is when I notice that Lock and Dam 15 has two lock chambers. I am very thankful, as it expedites my passage.

The days seem to be passing by very quickly. Yet when I study the calendar, it has only been twelve days since my departure. Preparing mentally for sixty, I realize I can look forward to many more days of adventure.

With tonight's camp set up on an island across from the small town of Buffalo, Iowa, it is time to catch up on some much needed rest.

Day 13

N. 41° 27' 04"
W. 90° 43' 09"

Refreshed by a good night's rest, I awake early, eager to discover what this new day will bring. *Who will I meet and what sights will I see from my small boat on the every increasing Mighty Mississippi?*

Several large, duck and goose blinds dot the river and its backwaters. While some are located on the banks and islands, others are situated right out in the river and not too far from the main channel. The locations are as diverse as their shapes and sizes. Most are big enough to drive a boat into them, each with a four-by-twelve-foot platform for the hunters to shoot from. Many of the blinds are covered in small willows for camouflage. Today's weather is as varied as the blinds, everything from bright sun to moderate rain. None of it lasts long though, so it is hard to get tired of one particular thing.

Once again I pass by Mark's campsite. He is probably still dreaming of tall mountains and wide oceans. He is camped on the opposite side of the river from me, so he must not have noticed me when he passed by last night.

I am rapidly approaching Lock and Dam 16 near Muscatine, Iowa. Now that larger commercial vessels congest the river more, I radio the lock when I am about a half-mile away. My plan is to use up some of my wait time by paddling. Expecting me to be nearby, the lockmaster asks, "Where are you? I can't see you." If I think he will be able to see me, I will wave my paddle; the flash of the blade can usually be detected clearly. If I am too far away, I will radio in my estimated time of arrival. This time I signal with my paddle and lock through in thirty minutes.

It seems each day I meet at least one person I can visit with, and today is no exception. It is late morning when I spot something traveling upstream toward me. With my binoculars, I spot a man paddling a small kayak. It doesn't take long to catch up to each other. We are equally happy to meet a fellow kayaker. Because he has a bunch of kayaking questions for me, he turns around and paddles downstream with me for a while.

Bob, from Fairfield, Iowa, often enjoys paddling on the river. Of course, I can relate. Bob is a tall, intelligent looking man having the same demeanor as the principal of our local high school back home.

After talking for about forty minutes about the river and paddling kayaks, Bob says, "I have something for you." He reaches into his coat pocket and pulls out a large, European chocolate bar. My mouth immediately begins to water. I graciously accept his gift, telling myself I will try to make it last for three days. I enjoy my surprise visit with Bob. He wishes me luck and we part, traveling in opposite directions once again.

Because of a ninety-minute wait before passing through Lock and Dam 17, I look for a place nearby to land and grab a quick meal. My only choice is a bank full of dense vegetation. I search for a small opening under tall trees. For lunch, I decide upon cold oatmeal with brown sugar. Both were portioned out in a Zip-Lock baggy before my trip began. I add about 2 cups of water and squish it around for a few moments. I am surprised at how delicious cold oatmeal is—like a liquid granola bar. *I wish I had packed more oatmeal.* Devouring lunch quickly, I close my eyes to catch a small nap.

I am close enough to the lock to hear the barge locking through. When I hear it leave, I make my way back to the kayak. The big barge passes within fifty yards of my location, so I allow its wake to lift my heavy boat. My radio is on and I wait for the lockmaster to tell me I can approach. At least ten minutes passes and nothing. I radio again and ask if it is now time to approach the lock.

To my dismay, the lockmaster responds, "Where are you Kayaker? I don't know anything about you? Are you north-bound or southbound?"

I reply back telling him I am southbound and have been waiting for almost two hours.

"Well, come on in," he says. "We just had a shift change and the previous shift did not tell us about you."

When I enter the lock chamber, two men come to talk with me for a few minutes. They tell me about two guys in a canoe who came through two days ago. Once the water subsides, they wish me good weather and I depart the lock. Talking to people who have an interest in my trip gives me a mental boost.

Two miles past Lock and Dam 17, I find a pristine, smooth sandbar. Just up the bank is a dense forest canopy. Under these large, soft maple trees is an ideal opening to set up my tent. One thing, though, makes this campsite unpleasant—bugs. They aren't the biting kind, just pesky. It seems hatching or mating season is in full swing. The bugs are a small 3/8-inch, light-colored moth. There are thousands of them and they are everywhere and on everything. I have to quickly cover my cockpit to keep them out of the kayak. I hurry to wash up, as they are getting all over me. They don't bite; they just crawl on me. I make a dash for my tent. They're not as thick in the trees as they are near the water's edge. In the diminishing light of the day, though, I can see them crawling on the outside of my tent. I am glad for my small shelter.

I realized something for the first time today. The kayak seat is not as comfortable and cushy as it was when I started. I'm not a big guy to begin with—5 foot, eight inches, 157 pounds—but today I am conscious of the fact that I am losing weight. *This isn't so bad, I guess.* With that, I drift off to sleep.

Day 14

N. 41° 09' 54"
W. 91° 01' 31"

Even though I sleep quite well, it seems each night I wake to the thought of somehow losing my kayak, either by someone messing with it, by the wind blowing it away, or by rising water gently stealing it from me. Even though I tie it down every time I leave it anywhere, I am haunted by the fact that it is still my only method of travel and I am so far from home. So, each night I find myself unzipping the tent to check on the kayak. It has always been there to this point, silently waiting to continue the long journey on this water trail.

As I approach consciousness this morning, I tell myself to sleep a little longer, giving my body some extra rest. I stay in the sleeping bag--not really sleeping--for a whole extra twelve minutes. I can't take it any longer; I have to get up.

This morning, like so many others, heavy dew blankets the exterior of my tent. This means I will stow it away wet. I hate this, because small patches of mildew are forming on the rain fly. There's not much I can do, though. This is just the way it is going to have to be. It is a cool morning and I am chilled wearing only a thin polar fleece vest as I roll up my sleeping bag and sleeping pad. I am warmed, however, with the excitement of what the new day will bring.

As I exit the tent, I feel dampness in the air and notice an easterly breeze. *I best get packed up quickly; there's a good chance of rain.*

After about an hour of paddling, to my surprise, the east wind dwindles to nothing and I paddle in what feels like a thick, heavy blanket. Not only does the air feel thick, but the water as well—like paddling in a river of pudding. *I just don't seem to be going very fast.* My GPS indicates this truth, also, as it clocks my speed at 3.7 miles per hour. I remind myself this trip isn't about speed. *Be thankful, I could have gale force head winds driving rain into my face. Pudding isn't so bad after all.*

Before 8:00 a.m., I notice a campground close to the river on the Illinois side. I need to top off my water, so I slide in quietly, get some water at a pump and slide right back out, without a soul seemingly knowing I was there. I am always relieved when I replenish my water supply. I can continue on for three days without the concern of needing anything.

As I continue on my way downstream, I spot a commercial fisherman's boat working its way up the east side. I check it out with the binoculars and notice they are using the round basket traps. I don't always stop to talk to commercial fisherman, because I realize they're very busy and have a lot of work to do for the day. But this time I am ready for a little conversation, and I secretly hope they are too. As the gap between our vessels decreases, it seems they, too, are willing to talk a bit. They motor near me as I paddle toward them. Speaking first, I ask, "You catching any?"

"Yeah, some," says the older of the two, who has a long white beard like Santa Claus. The younger one, probably in his mid-twenties, has a small, scraggily beard. Both are wearing rain gear and the name on the side of their aluminum boat 'OQUAWKA' seems to be the brand name.

"Channel or flathead?" I strain to see their catch.

"Both."

"I don't see many catfish up where I'm from," I reply with a smile.

"Where you from?" one asks.

"Prescott, Wisconsin."

The younger fisherman pokes around in the big catch box that holds the fish.

"Watch out, you don't get stung," the older fellow says.

"Do they really sting?" I ask.

"Oh yeah. It hurts, too," the young guy answers as he pulls out two big catfish, one of each kind. After a few seconds he drops them back in.

"How do you like that there kayak?" quizzes the older fellow.

"Really well."

"That's pretty small and you're a long way from home."

I ask them how their fishing season goes during high waters.

"We do good in high water," the young fisherman proclaims. "We caught cats when the water was way up in those trees." He points to the wooded riverbanks. "Nobody else is catching much except us. The high water doesn't hurt us at all."

As long as I have their attention, I ask for a news update on the terrorist attacks on the World Trade Center.

The young guy is quick to reply, "Well, have you heard the latest? We're about to dee-clare war on Argentina."

Wow! This is bigger than I had first anticipated. "Argentina? I didn't know South America was involved in this. Are you sure you don't mean Afghanistan?"

The young guy pauses thoughtfully, "Yeah, maybe you're right. I believe it is Afghanistan."

The older fisherman adds, "That's one big mistake they made. When they attacked the World Trade Center, they attacked all peoples, nationalities and religions. Why, they even killed their own kind," he responds with a very sure and determined look on his face,

"Someone will pay big!" adds the younger guy.

The older gentleman says, "I'm not so sure going to war is the right thing to do, though." The look on his face says his mind is somewhere else—maybe a place and a time where there was pain and suffering of innocent people. *Has this man seen war firsthand?*

As a kid, my dad never let me watch war movies on TV. He said, "Son, you just don't realize the evil side of war and all the hatred that is involved in it." *Does this commercial fisherman see war like my dad did?*

To change the heavy subject, I ask permission to take their picture.

The white-bearded man responds, "Well, I don't know why you'd ever want to see me again."

"I'm taking pictures of everyone I meet and talk to on this trip and I would like to take one of you guys, if it's okay?" They consent. I take a picture of them each holding a catfish.

"You be careful down this big river and good luck," wishes the older fisherman. I thank them for the picture and wish them good fishing. We slowly drift apart. I am grateful for the meeting.

After about an hour of paddling in the heavy air, I notice swallows, lots of them, skimming above the surface of the water. *I wonder if they are some of the same I have seen further up the river in Wisconsin.* They glide effortlessly within four to six feet of me. I can see their small heads turn and look at me as they float past. They seem as intrigued with me as I am with them. *How nice it would be to have wings, sailing over land and water.*

Near Oquawka, Illinois, I can hear a motorboat behind me. It slows and approaches. Quickly, I snap on my spray skirt, in case there are waves. I turn to look as it approaches on my left. A man standing behind the controls talks loud over the noise of his motor.

."I got a friend I knew in the service. He said he was going to go down the river." Looking at me carefully he adds, "You're not him. I'll keep my eyes open."

I didn't have to say a word. He pulls back into the main channel and speeds off.

I continue paddling past Oquawka and approach Lock and Dam 18. As usual, I radio ahead. I watch for the light before entering. There is no flashing light, but only a command to advance over the radio. I can see a barge approaching the lock from the south. I figure they want to hurry me through. When the gates are three quarters open, I paddle in. *The wrong thing to do, I guess.*

The lockmaster shouts angrily, "Go over to the wall and I'll give you a rope."

By the time I get there, he is waiting for me. He scolds me for approaching too close to the lock doors. I argue that I was given permission to approach over the radio.

"Don't get close until you get the signal."

"What signal?" I asked, "radio, lights, horn?"

Every lock seems to be different. Some signal multiple ways and some only one. He drops me a rope while continuing his lecture.

I look straight ahead and keep repeating, "Yes, Sir."

As I leave the lock, I wave politely to the man and say, "Thanks."

He doesn't respond. *He must really be mad at me for taking up his lock time with my little kayak. I will be more cautious in the future.*

The bird I see most often is the great Blue Heron. I see at least one every mile or so. Today is no exception. I know they subsist off fish, but I've never actually seen one catch a fish until today. I pass within thirty feet of one standing as still as something frozen solid in time. The only thing that moves is the small three- to four-inch fish, wiggling and squirming as it hangs by its tail. The heron patiently waits until the fish becomes still. With one quick movement, the bird gulps the fish whole. *I guess these birds don't have taste buds to enjoy flavor like we humans do.* It's always nice to see things in nature that aren't always common place.

The Blue Heron reminds me of an interesting site I observed while living in Alaska:

> *My brother and I were camped far back in the foothills of eastern Alaska on the open tundra. We awoke early one morning, and as always on that trip, looked out the tent, for we never knew what we might see. We could*

see for miles in every direction. To the south-east was a small pond about a half-mile away.

As we looked down onto the lake, that beautiful Alaskan morning, we noticed movement in the pond. It was a cow moose swimming in the lake with what appeared to be two small calves. I reached for my spotting scope to get a closer look. As I zoomed .in, everything changed. No longer was it a cow moose swimming peacefully with her young calves, but rather a life and death scenario playing out before our eyes. What I thought were two young moose were actually two wolves aggressively trying to attack the big cow moose. I knew from prior experience, that where there were one or two wolves, there were more. I scanned the banks of the pond. As I thought, two more wolves, on opposite sides of the pond. They were crouched down, waiting for the two wolves in the water to chase the moose onto ground where they would have a better chance of a successful kill.

The moose had the advantage in the water as her long legs enabled her to run in the three- to four-foot deep pond. The wolves, on the other hand, were forced to swim. Back and forth, back and forth, the moose went, not wanting to leave the safety of the water. The two wolves on the bank remained hidden. Eventually, the two swimming wolves tired and headed for shore. As soon as the wolves gave up the chase and left the area, the moose took off in the opposite direction. Wow, what a sight seldom seen in nature.

I pass by a housing area today. The riverbanks are lined up with houses on stilts. Some are eight feet up and some are as high as twenty feet off the ground. This, I assume, enables the inhabitants to weather the many floods that plague the river. This stilted housing area goes on for several miles. There aren't many people around that I can see. The houses look abandoned—all quiet, no cars moving about, no kids playing, and no activity of any kind. It is as if I am the only person alive. This makes me want to call Wendi and Isaac. It has been about six days since I have heard their voices. Tomorrow I will look for a small town to call them from.

I continue to paddle until about 4:00 p.m. I find an inviting camping area with a high sand bank. It plateaus as it meets the trees. After securing the kayak, I set up the tent. I put a small pot of rice on the stove to cook. While supper is cooking, I unload my kayak, spreading the damp gear out to dry. By this time, the rice is ready and I am hungry. As I'm putting away the clean dishes, I notice the book Gordy, the commercial fisherman, gave me. It is a little wet and has some sand on the cover from traveling with me the last four days. *Is it worth packing along any more? If Gordy is kind enough to give it to me, I can at least*

A hot meal served river style.

look it over before discarding it. I read the title, *When Hell Was in Session.* Turning to the back cover, I discover it is a biography about Senator Jeremiah Denton during the time when he was a prisoner of war in Vietnam. I hear Gordy's last words replay in my head, "Don't quit. Keep going until you make it to the end. Just don't quit." Gordy gave me this book as an encouragement. There are times on the river when I am sore, tired, cold and wet, yet these don't even compare to what the prisoners of war went through. *Denton didn't quit and neither will I.* I resolve to read the entire book and keep it as an encouragement and a reminder of Gordy, the setline fisherman, who cared enough about me, a stranger paddling down the Mississippi River. Thanks Gordy.

Day 15

N. 40° 45' 06"
W. 91° 06' 06"

At this point, fourteen days into my trip, I have no idea how many more days it will take to finish. I can only estimate. When traveling by myself, estimations are but a fragile guess. Some days I am overwhelmed with the possibility of tragedy causing my adventure to end. I try not to dwell on that; but the thought gives me a good doze of caution from time to time.

It is 6:50 a.m. before I am back in the cockpit of my faithful kayak. *Slacker!* Actually, I needed the extra down time. I had come thirty-five miles the previous day and almost every bit of it in a soaking rain. It was very draining on the mind and body.

Ahead lies the challenge of a very wide and long Pool 19 and a 36-foot drop at Keokuk, Iowa.

I find a marina in Fort Madison, Iowa, to make a call to Wendi, passing on GPS coordinates. I purchase three pops from a machine, figuring I can save the plastic bottles to collect water, if need be.

Like yesterday, I find myself paddling along the eastern bank, which offers me more protection from wind. The clouds hang heavy, like a water balloon about to burst. At 9:30 a.m. a light rain begins to fall. Within ninety minutes the rain comes down in a steady shower, similar to yesterday. Until this time, I have been able to stay fairly dry under my rain suit and spray skirt.

I am enjoying my time paddling in the rain; then I hear something. I am not sure what it is. I hear it again and look back to see a fellow on shore waving both hands. Because of the rain, I cannot hear what he is shouting and I don't want to paddle upstream to find out. I politely wave and keep going. *Is he being friendly or warning me of danger?*

On days like this, I am very careful to watch out for lightning. At the first sound of thunder, I head for land to think the situation over. Today, even though it is thickly overcast and raining, there hasn't been a rumble of thunder. I feel pretty safe paddling in these conditions.

Most of Navoo, Illinois, is situated beyond the high bank, making it difficult to see and calculate its actual size. After passing Navoo State Park, fog sets in, obscuring my view of the opposite river bank. I am having difficulty spotting most channel markers. I choose to continue paddling the Illinois side avoiding a blind crossing—a futile decision. The Mississippi River is now the

Mississippi Marsh. Paddling in weeds makes for a long day and few miles. I spy two fisherman in a boat anchored ahead of me. The fog enhances my stealthy approach.

"You guys are some pretty hard-core fishermen—being out in this rain." Both heads snap toward me.

They look at me like I'm a two-headed monster and say nothing.

I guess I'll have to ask these two a question in order to get a conversation going. "This side of the river is shallow and weedy. What's the other side like?"

"The deep channel is on that side." One man points west. "Where'd you come from?"

"Wisconsin. I'm heading to the Gulf."

"That's a long way. You'd better get going."

Sensing this conversation isn't going to develop, I wish them good fishing and paddle off.

Now I have a dilemma—stick to the safe side with weeds or cross the river in the rain and fog to the deep channel, risking a collision with a boat or barge? I prepare to cross over. My ears will be my primary protection. I ease my kayak out, drifting quietly for at least a minute. I listen intently for any noise that might signal danger. I hear nothing but the little splatters of rain as they hit my kayak.

Well, if I'm going to go, I'd better go quickly. I take one last look at the map and estimate a distance of 200-300 yards to the other bank. I propel forward with a strong power stroke. At midpoint, I stop paddling for one more sound check. All seems clear at first, then suddenly, I hear the dull drone of a diesel engine. *I must get to the other side quickly now!* Stroke,

stroke. Adrenaline shoots through my body. My eyes feverishly search for the protection of the opposite bank. Finally, I spot the faint outline of shore. Paddle, paddle. *I'm going to make it!* Dig, dig. Reaching the other side, I look back in time to view a barge passing through the area I had just sprinted through. *Thank you, God, for strength and protection!*

For the next ten miles, I stay within view of the Iowa shore. I have been in the kayak for about six hours now and need to get out to stretch my legs, but there's a problem. A railroad track now parallels the river, which usually means riprap shorelines. I guess I'll have to continue on just as the rain continues on. This will be another opportunity to practice for when I get down in Louisiana and can't find a place to stop in those big swamps. I retrieve a Power Bar from my deck bag to keep me going.

An observation I made while paddling the upper half of the Mississippi is that wherever there was a train track close to the water, landings and launchings were difficult. Those unfriendly shores, made of jagged rocks, scratched and gouged my craft's hull. The wave action of the water only added to the treachery. Either I had to lift the boat all the way out of the water—*how easy was that when it weighed close to 150 pounds*—or I kept going.

The upper part of the river, especially along the Wisconsin, Minnesota, Iowa, and Illinois borders, had many railroads near the water's edge. It was good to look for sandy islands. Sometimes the opposite shores were favorable, unless there were tracks on both sides, as was the case with the lower half of Lake Pepin. If I couldn't find a resting place along the banks, then small towns, like Wabasha, Minnesota, and Pepin, Wisconsin, were my best bet until I reached more islands.

As I approach Lock and Dam 19 at Keokuk, on the southern border of Iowa, it is still raining hard and constant. Instead of digging my radio out, I decide to pull the small boat cord signal. I pull and wait. No response. I pull it again and still nothing. Finally, a lock worker notices me and comes over.

"I pulled the cord two times hard," I say, "but I got no response." He is surprised it didn't work and says he will inform the lockmaster I am here.

Lock and Dam 19 has the greatest drop—thirty-six feet—of all the locks I have been through. The doors of the lock close behind me encasing me in a huge watery tomb. There are no ropes to hold; only huge metal bobbers raise and drop with the water level.

Before my decent, I ask the lock attendant if there are any sandbars within the next mile or so. He says the only one he knows of is about ten miles downstream.

"Too far!" I tell him. "I have already come 35 miles."

He thinks for a moment. "Well, there may be a small, sandy area just past the dam on the Illinois side. I'm not sure."

That will have to do. The water begins to lower inside the lock and so do the big, metal floats. The screeching and howling of metal rubbing against metal adds to the spookiness of this tomb-like lock. The sky is dark and eerie. I've come a long way in the pouring rain. I'm tired, cold and wet. I long for the shelter and warmth of my tent and sleeping bag. Finally, the gates open and I make my way out.

As soon as I pass the lock wall, I turn left and head directly for the far shore, negotiating the strong, swirling current caused by the release of large volumes of water. I ferry across, catching eddies to hold my position behind the bridge pillars.

It is a relief to nudge the bow of my kayak onto the muddy shore under the bridge. *At least I'm out of the rain. I guess this just might be home for the night.* Stepping out of the kayak, my foot sinks past my ankle into the gooey mud. I take another long step, my other foot sinking. I jump a couple more times onto a grassy strip. It's still muddy, but better.

I explore this unfamiliar place before actually deciding to lay my head down for the night. The tall bridge enables the wind to blow the rain beneath it. I spy one dry area up under the middle of the bridge, where the rocks and dirt meet. I am careful not to fall or twist an ankle while negotiating the basketball-sized rocks. Getting all the way under the bridge, I discover it to be bone dry. *This is good. Graffiti and weird writings painted on the cement underside of the bridge is not. Is this a safe place to be for the night?* I look around a little more to make sure. I notice a small object on a large, metal beam. It's a disposable camera. *Maybe it was used to photograph the artists in action. Will its owners be coming back to retrieve it? If they brave the weather, hopefully they will be as afraid of me as I would be of them. I have to make a decision—go back out in the pouring rain and dimming light to look for another place or take my chances under this bridge? The bridge it is.*

Wearing my headlamp, I sit down on a rock to journal and enjoy the last half of a chocolate bar. Beside me I keep my rain suit and VHF marine radio. NOAA Weather Radio forecasts more moderate rains throughout the night, rains diminishing by morning and cloudy weather tomorrow. *I'm looking forward to that. I may sleep on these rocks, eliminating the need to set up the tent in the muddy grass below. I will wear the headlamp through the night, so if I should have a visitor, I can turn it on quickly.*

It is hard to fall asleep, so for a long while, I lay back with my eyes open. It is now almost totally dark. My eye glimpses a small shadowy object running between my kayak and me. I quickly flip on my headlamp. The shadow stops and two silvery eyes peer my way. *What is that? Probably a coon.* After a ten-second stare down, it takes off running for the woods. The sight of animals has never bothered me. I know they are trying to survive out here like I am.

I am beginning to get somewhat sleepy now and put my head back. As I am dozing, something runs across my face. I brush it away. It happens again, and then again. I look around with my light, noticing hundreds of spiders coming out from under the rocks. Mosquitoes are beginning to pester me as well. *Maybe they'll go away if I ignore them—maybe not.* Mosquitoes are biting my hands and buzzing in my ears; spiders are scurrying across my face—*I've had enough. I guess I'll have to pitch my tent in the mud after all.* I pick out the best spot to set up a minimal camp—tent and sleeping bag, that's it. What a delight to crawl into my warm, dry sleeping bag, free of pesky insects.

Day 16

N. 40° 23' 22"
W. 91° 22' 12"

The night seemed long, as I was awakened by the wind and rain several times. And, of course, I had to get up at least once to check the kayak. Chalk it all up—the rain, the mud, the danger, the critters, and the restless sleep—as part of the adventure.

Morning doesn't come soon enough and I am up in the early darkness packing away my tent and sleeping bag. The headlamp, rather than a hand-held flashlight, works perfect for times like these. It frees up both hands and wherever I look, the light is there with me. I make a check on the map. Two more miles and "Good-bye Iowa! Hello Missouri!"

As I paddle, the morning light makes a feeble attempt to pierce the heavy, cloud cover. However, it's not raining, and I'm thankful for that. Objects are faint in the distance.

Now in Missouri, I notice movement on the riverbank. A family of five river otters entertains me with their chirping and playing in and out of the water. River otters appear to have a good life. They are skillful hunters and never seem to be starving for food. Slowly, I drift by. They stop playing and take notice. They begin to make otter sounds, as if they are inviting me join the fun.

In the early afternoon I hear a drumming sound. A lone fish, about eight inches long, flops wildly on my rear hatch cover trying to escape. In a few seconds, he flops into the river, vanishing as quickly as he appeared.

After passing through Lock and Dam 20, I begin looking for a place to stop for the night. An island with a sand bank affords enough room for my tent. Not the best campsite I've had, but anything's better than last night's. The best sandy sites seem to be just beyond the locks. The farther away I get, the harder it is to find a good spot to camp. Even though this is true, my favorite campsites are the ones I had the first week.

The island is located one mile from a small town on the eastern bank. I can see a few buildings poking up from behind a levee. Faintly, I hear the beating of drums and music of a band—a high school marching band. It reminds me of crisp, fall evenings listening to the far-off sounds of the Prescott High School Marching Band entertaining the Cardinal football fans with their half-time shows.

A small town is a good place to raise a family, I think. Some say there's not much to do. I say there are less distractions and interruptions. Small towns seem to be focused on school and family. I am glad I grew up in the country about seven miles from a small town like the one across the river, where the simple things in life were important and fun. I can remember as a tiny boy having a hand pump in our house. If we needed water, we didn't go to the faucet; we went to the pump. I guess the point is, that as a kid I didn't feel like I was missing out in life by having to pump water. Like now, I don't miss having a big boat with all its luxuries to take me down the river. I am very content with my simple kayak. It doesn't require spark plugs or gas and it will take me into places the big boats can't go.

It's time to do laundry. I'm still trying to remove the purple ring from my T-shirt. The wind is blowing fairly strong; my wet clothes should dry quickly.

I haven't seen the sun much this past week—I don't mind. The reflection of the sunlight on the water is very strenuous on my eyes. I don't even mind an occasional rain shower. What I'm not fond of is continuous rain day after day. Tomorrow the weatherman predicts a fifty percent chance of rain.

My food and water supplies are holding out well. Oh, I stop now and then for the occasional treat to appease my cravings, but as for need, I've brought more than enough food.

On this section of the river, wing dams are not prevalent. Neither is the river's current as swift as I had hoped it would be. This may change below St. Louis, when all the locks and dams are no more.

Today I paddled twenty-two miles. Tomorrow I will do more. My body is performing excellently. No soreness plagues my back or shoulders.

I pick up my journal for the second time tonight. Retiring early gives me more time to record my adventures. It is now 6:30 p.m., an hour before dark. This is the hardest part of the day for me. I tend to reflect my thoughts toward home and family. *What would I be doing if I were home tonight? Maybe Wendi, Isaac and I would be on a bike ride, or maybe I'd be watching Isaac's football game, or maybe we'd be relaxing together as a family.* Sometimes I think we underestimate the importance of family until it's gone.

When I see or do something funny while paddling, it seems I never laugh. If I were with my family, though, we would really laugh. As our son grows older, he makes Wendi and me laugh more and more. When he was a tiny baby we made him laugh. Now he is always cracking jokes or making up silly songs. I love to laugh, but it's different when I'm alone.

Isaac is becoming a strong young man and I see so many positive things in him. Many months before I took this trip, I talked a lot about doing it. When Isaac said to me, "Dad, you won't do it," in some ways, he challenged me. I feel that a man should be good to his word. If I say I will do something, then I will do all I can to carry out my word. I'm not embarking on this trip to prove to him I am man enough, but rather to show him that I am true to my word. I am proud of my son, very proud, and I hope to pass on to him true integrity.

As a small child, my dad used to tell me, "Son, just remember, half the blood running through your body is from me." My dad was saying that after he passed away, I would be the living legacy that he left behind in this world. This is true with my son, too. I tell him the blood thing and that I love him very much.

The sun is about to spread its last rays of light over my small river world. Thoughts of my family linger as this sixteenth day on the river comes to a close. Even though many miles separate me from my wife and son, our hearts are still joined. *I love you both!*

Day 17

N. 40° 07' 05"
W. 91° 30' 17"

Because I cashed in a little prematurely yesterday, I am up and ready to go by 5:00 a.m. I stay close to the bank as I slowly paddle in the last thirty minutes of darkness, listening to the pre-dawn sounds of the river—owls hooting, fish flopping and even beautiful silence. Some people feel uneasy with silence. I love it and look forward to quiet times.

The farther south I travel, the less sport traffic I encounter. The river's purpose has transformed from recreational to commercial. Maybe it's just the time of year.

It's time to replenish the water supply; Quincy, Illinois, might be a good place for this. I never know from one town to the next whether its river access is friendly or not. I approach Quincy with anticipation. Workers wearing orange vests and hard hats mill about on the high bridge that crosses the river at Quincy. They seem so far up and I feel so small. One worker points down at me. The whole crew stops working and peers down at my small floating craft. I wave enthusiastically and they return the gesture. I like it when people wave back. It's an encouraging boost. They keep looking and I keep paddling.

I make my way over to the Quincy shoreline. A pleasant park borders the river—just what I like to see. I peer through my binoculars looking for a water source. I see a man watering plants with a garden hose—perfect. I find a place to hop out and tie up the Gulfstream. Grabbing my empty water containers I make my way up the bank. I hope no one falsely labels me as river trash and boots me out of this elegantly manicured park. The Bible says that kind words turn away wrath and that's what I intend to use. After all, I'm the visitor, and a kind word can never hurt.

I approach the man with the hose. "Good morning, Sir."

"Morning," he responds.

"I was wondering," I begin, eyeing up the cold, clear water flowing from the end of the hose, "if that water is good for drinking?"

"Sure is," the kind man replies. "Do you need some?"

"I sure do, Sir." I tell him briefly about my trip and he shows genuine enthusiasm for my endeavor.

"Here, let me turn it down a little for you." Don updates me on the terrorist attacks, as well as the local economy of Quincy.

Wishing he had something else to give me, he inquires, "Do you need any toilet paper?" Because I have plenty at this time, I graciously turn down his kind gesture.

"I'd like to come down to the river to see your boat."

"Sure, come on down," I reply. By the time we reach the boat, we have covered everything from employment to marriage to drowning in the Mississippi.

When he sees my red kayak tied to the bank he comments, "Wow! That's a real nice setup."

"It sure is working out good." Before popping back into the river, I fish out my camera to snap his picture.

"Take care, Byron." I am off, feeling privileged to have met Don.

The weather is beginning to deteriorate. NOAA Weather Radio doesn't have much good to say about it either. There are two things I want to do before stopping for the day. First, I want to reach Hannibal, Missouri, and second, to set up camp before it begins to rain. To do both will take a valiant effort from my body.

Making fast work of Lock and Dam 21, I begin with a quick, strong stoke. I am able to maintain the pace for several hours, ticking the miles off quickly. My arms and back hold out like troopers as I close in on my goals. As I pass under the bridge at Hannibal, I look intently for a campsite. I can see thunderheads forming behind me. It is 4:00 p.m. and I figure I have less than fifteen minutes before the storm breaks. *There! An island with a sandbar, the perfect spot.* I make haste for the island; I have no time to waste.

Anticipating a tornado, I set the tent up in quick fashion between two half-sunken drift logs, anchoring each tie-down—a total of sixteen—securely. In goes the sleeping bag and pad. All I can do is wait and hope. By 4:30 p.m. rain is pouring down, thunder is booming and vicious lightning is cutting up the sky. Here I lay in my fragile tent near the birthplace of Mark Twain, the man who made the Mississippi River famous. Surely, Tom Sawyer and Huck Finn survived storms like this.

By 7:17 p.m. the worst of the storm is over and I decide I need some nourishment. I rummage through the scanty supplies I had managed to throw into the tent before the storm. *Ah, trail mix and oatmeal, just what I need!* Even simple foods taste like a delicacy at times like this. Soon after my stomach is full, I drift off to sleep, despite the thunder and lightning still playing war in the distance.

Day 18

N. 39° 42' 53"
W. 91° 20' 47"

Exiting the tent, I notice the stars are out. It is clear and cool, but not cold. Surprisingly, the wind is blowing down river. *What a bonus!* I truly enjoy the ease of paddling with the breeze at my back—a contrast to the last night's tempest. Now I enjoy the warmth of the rising sun as it causes the dampness of night to surrender its grip on the river and its banks.

Today will bring me through Locks 22 and 24. There is no Lock 23. Apparently plans were drawn up for the construction of Lock and Dam 23, but later it was determined that Lock and Dam 24 could lift fifteen feet of water instead of the planned ten feet, eliminating the need for Lock and Dam 23.

Even though I replenished my water supply yesterday in Quincy, I feel the need to top off my containers today, if possible. I'm not sure if I'll be able to get water again until St. Louis, which could be at least four days out. I consider the lock facilities for water, but it is getting more difficult to land, as the southern locks are not as small-boat friendly as the northern locks. I pass through Lock and Dam 22 without stopping for water.

Mid-morning I notice movement on the Missouri shore. Along the bank, a red fox is hunting for a tasty morsel of food. He doesn't notice me. The fox steps lightly, sniffing each log.or rock that may hide a meal. I observe its every move as I drift parallel, forty yards out from shore. We continue together for two hundred yards until the fox fades into the dense brush.

As noon approaches, I paddle closer to shore looking for a spot to get out to stretch and have lunch. In front of me I see what looks like a turtle's head breaking the surface of the water three feet from shore. As I drift closer, though, it looks less like a turtle's head. It sticks up higher and is more slender, and it doesn't disappear like turtles normally do when approached. Now five feet away, I realize it's a water snake. *Why here and why now, when I need to get out of my boat?* I can see its piercing, black eyes lock onto me. It did not move. This snake gives me the creeps. I jab my paddle at it. Slowly, it disappears into the water.

There's quite a bit of mud and shoreline growth, including poison ivy, on this part of the river. Carefully, I nose the bow of my kayak onto shore. Warily I eat my shore lunch, keeping an eye open for Mr. Evil Eye Snake. In less than twenty minutes I am back on the river, happy to be paddling.

Up ahead, Louisiana, Missouri. With the help of my binoculars I scope out the river town. Like Quincy, a park borders the Mississippi River. Hoping it has water, I paddle over to a small dock and notice a man watching me.

"Good day!" I yell.

He cups his hand to his ear, "I can't hear you. I'll come down there."

I pull my kayak up on the shore. Turning to the man, I ask, "Can you show me where I can get some water?" I used to ask, "Is there any place I can get water around here?" People would point in the general direction of town, leaving me just as unsure as before I asked. Deciding to make the question more personal, I now ask to be shown. This works much better.

"Where'd you come from?"

"Prescott, Wisconsin," I reply.

"Way up there; in that skinny little boat? Are you all by yourself?"

"Yes, Sir," I tell him.

"Aren't you scared?"

"Well, not really. What should I be scared of?"

"Snakes and big boats and stuff. Boy, you're a better man than me. I'd be scared," is his answer. "I'll take you to some water."

I introduce myself and we shake hands.

"I'm Jesse. That's Jesse with an 'E', not an 'IE', 'cause that's the way the girls spell it." Jesse is a true gentleman. He is kind and courteous. As we go for water, he yells out to some other people in the park, "Hey, this here fellow came all the way from Wisconsin paddling a kayak." He points toward the river.

Remembering out loud, I tell Jesse, "I forgot to tie my boat down."

"It'll be fine," he says.

"But a wake or something might set it afloat."

Jesse hollers to an older fellow, "Hey, go watch this boy's boat for him and don't let it float away." The man does as Jesse instructs, making me feel at ease.

We walk a hundred yards to a somewhat hidden water spigot. "I saw a guy use this one time before, so I knew it was here."

Once again my water containers are full and I can relax, for a while anyway. As we return to the boat, Jesse tells me of a bicyclist who once came through on a long trip. "I gave him my address and he wrote to me a few months later. I'll give you my address, too. Let me know you make it okay." I write down Jesse's address, and he poses for a picture next to my kayak. Wearing a plaid shirt and with hands on his hips, Jesse with an "E" cocks his head and smiles for the camera. Once again, thankful for the kind gesture and a full water supply, I nudge the kayak out into the river's current.

Today there's very little boat traffic. I continue to paddle in relative quiet with the slight breeze still at my back. All is well. My body is becoming conditioned to the constant paddling, I'm no longer bothered by shoulder pain and my hands are callusing in all the right places.

At 4:00 p.m. I approach Lock and Dam 24. I radio the lockmaster as usual. In a couple of minutes the gates open. Now inside, the lockmaster comes over to greet me, "Was that you that just radioed me? I was expecting a larger boat."

I've paddled forty miles today and tell him that I'm looking for a campsite.

"We have a little park you can camp at right here in Clarksville," the lockmaster suggests. "There's a little store up the street where you can get food or whatever you need. There are rest rooms in the park." *Camping in Clarksville, Missouri, sounds like a good idea to me.*

It feels good to shave and wash up even though the water is cold. I realize I have not showered in eighteen days. At least nothing's growing on my skin, yet, and I haven't been sick.

Now presentable, I walk into the small town. I have come 500 miles, so I decide to treat myself; my taste buds are celebrating! I savor a pop and a slice of hot pizza for as long as possible. *As good as they taste, I best get back to the park to set up camp.* I pick a location near my kayak. I am troubled because the bank is steep and I can't see the kayak from my tent. I'll have to trust all will be okay.

I write in my journal—*it was a good day. The sun was shining throughout. It was eighty degrees today. If it's in the eighties in late September, what's it like in the heat of summer? Too hot for me, I'm sure. Tomorrow I hope for cooler temperatures.*

As I continue writing and fiddling with my GPS, a young man—in his late teens to early twenties—slowly works his way toward me, throwing rocks into the river along the way.

"How's it going?" I ask, when he gets to within ten yards of me.

"All right," he responds with a drawl. "Where you from?"

"I paddled that kayak all the way from Wisconsin," I say with enthusiasm.

"Hmm," is his response.

"How big is this town?" I ask.

"Oh, I'm not sure. But we don't have any cops, because the town can't afford any."

Great. A town without the law.

A passing vehicle squeals its tires. "See that blue truck?" The man points his thumb over his shoulder. "That's the third one she's had this year. She keeps smashin' 'em up, then gets a different one."

Kenny's a local boy. He wears a black T-shirt and blue jeans. A chain connects his wallet, protruding from the back pocket, to a belt loop.

"Have you ever been out of Missouri?" I ask him.

"Once I was in Arkansas," he says, "but I got out of there. Those people are weird!"

Kenny and I talk sporadically for another thirty minutes or so.

A tow motors up the river and stops along the Clarksville riverbank. "I think I'll go see what that barge is up to." Kenny wanders off.

I gather up my gear and shove it into the tent. I check on my kayak before retiring for the night.

As darkness settles in, Clarksville comes alive. I hear more squealing tires, and not far from my tent, people fish throughout the night. One guy talks loudly and I hear most of his conversation about how to catch catfish "in these here parts," and why his way is better than everyone else's. *Well, I don't know much about fishing for catfish, but I do know that at 2:00 a.m., I'm dog-tired.*

Finally, at 3:30 a.m. all seems quiet. I slip out of the tent to have a peek at my kayak. I am glad to see her resting patiently right where I put her. I sneak back to the tent and slide into my warm sleeping bag. *Can I power sleep for two hours?*

Day 19

N. 39° 22' 18"
W. 90° 54' 13"

Packing up at 5:30, I've had all I can take of Clarksville, Missouri. I'm hoping for a peaceful paddle today since there are no towns to speak of until Alton, Illinois.

Starting out in a thick wall of fog, I cling to the Missouri bank. I paddle with all my senses on high alert. Because there are many islands in this stretch of the river, I watch the map closely, being careful not to drift accidentally into the main channel and in front of some massive piece of moving steel.

I hear the low moan of a giant diesel engine. *Is it moving or parked on my side of the river?* Often times, in the fog, barges will park alongside the riverbank—this is the good news. The bad news is, I usually have to paddle out into the channel to get around them, never knowing when they'll come to life. I'm like Jack waking the giant in *Jack and the Beanstalk*—not a good situation to be in.

I approach the noise cautiously, preparing to sprint to one side or the other. Not until there's only fifteen yards between us, do I see a towering tow with several barges parked against the shore. I will have to go around. Allowing the current to take me downstream, I perform sculling draw strokes to move me vertically out around the beast. I pass at a close distance of fifteen feet, not wanting to go too far into the middle of the river. I notice three people on the deck of the tow, two of which are dressed in white and wearing chefs hats.

"Good morning!" I yell. "You won't run me over will you?"

Three heads snap in my direction, their eyes wide like they've seen a ghost. "No, we'll watch out for you," one crewmember says.

Looking up into the control room, I see a man looking down on me. I wave; he waves back. Comforted by the fact that the captain is aware of my presence, I continue on confidently, my arms pumping like two pistons on a mechanical engine.

An hour later, the sun's rays cut through the fog. Today is Saturday and many recreational boats will be out in full force, stirring up the river, making it jiggly.

The river is widening greatly, and the water's current seems to be slowing. These are both indicators of a lock and dam. Ahead I notice a US Army Corps of Engineers channel dredging system, taking up about one-third of the river. This large piece of equipment is very important for the commercial traffic on the river. It keeps the main channel open at least to nine feet deep. Not only that, but it pumps out millions of pounds of sand from the bottom of the main channel creating beautiful sandbars along the riverbanks.

About the time I am engrossed with watching the dredging operation, around the bend comes a stately looking riverboat. Since I have to move toward the main channel to get around the dredging equipment, I paddle to within fifty yards of the American Queen. At 418 feet, it is the largest of all riverboats.

As people begin congregating on her decks, I get out my camera to take a couple of photos. Shortly, several more people gather to take my picture. How ironic. Here I am amazed with the enormity of their boat as they marvel at my insignificance; yet both of us use the same waterway—the great and mighty Mississippi. Other pleasure boats gather, capturing the passengers' attention; this is my cue to leave.

I move down the ever-widening channel, not sure which side I want to be on. I prefer to position myself on the same side as an upcoming lock, but this isn't always possible as the wind may drive me to the opposite side to seek relief. Today, the bank opposite the lock offers the best protection from the wind.

I paddle across the channel just in time to let a north-bound sailboat, under motor power, slide by my stern at a safe distance. Making two more bends in the river, Lock and Dam 25, about three miles away, comes into view. Disappointingly, I also notice five barges waiting to lock through. As you know, I'm not fond of portaging, but because I'm not excited about waiting six hours, I will give in this time.

I point my bow toward the spillway, just to the left of the dam. It is 2:00 p.m. and the wind has calmed. I make my way across the glassy water. Just then I caught a flash of something zipping across the surface of the water. A water spider, traveling three miles per hour, hops onto my kayak. I don't care for spiders—never have, never will. Maybe he's looking for a dry spot to take a break, or maybe he's running from a big old catfish; whatever the reason, I don't want him on my kayak. Climbing to within six feet of me, I splash water on him with my paddle, knocking him off. I focus again on the spillway. Here comes another spider scuttling along the mirror-like surface of the water—then another. *What's up with this?* In all, I see about a dozen water-skimming spiders within two miles of the spillway. After the first, I never let another catch a ride.

Within the past hour I have seen the largest riverboat and the tiniest water spider. What's interesting to me is that all three of us can share the same water.

Searching for a good spot to get out, I pull my kayak onto the cement spillway about a hundred feet in front of the dam. I scout ahead to find the best path to portage to the other side. It doesn't take me long to discover there is no trail; I will have to pick my way through 150 yards of brush and weeds to a muddy spot on the other side. Returning to my kayak, a pontoon boat carrying seven middle-aged men pulls up to my kayak.

"Need any help portaging?" one asks.

His offer is tempting, but I graciously decline, not wanting to impose on their fishing time.

"Well, how about a drink of something cold then?" another asks.

It's at least eighty degrees and my throat is dry. I know water is the best thirst quencher, but I can't refuse a cold drink. They fish in the cooler, pulling out a two ice cold Cokes. I down the first in less than a minute and save the second.

The men return to their fishing, and I begin the task of portaging. Watching for snakes, it takes me three trips and forty-five minutes to safely portage my gear and kayak across. *See why I like locking through better? One, it's much easier—I don't have to lug my boat and equipment around; the water carries me through. Two, it's much safer—there's no risk of a twisted ankle or broken bone. Three, it's much quicker—granted the wait may be longer (I can always do other important tasks in the meantime), but the lock process takes about twenty minutes.* Thankfully, of the twenty-two dams I have encountered this far, I've locked through twenty of them.

I soon realize a significant increase in the small boat traffic on the other side of Lock and Dam 25. Well, they're considered "small", but most are much larger than my kayak. This is the first time in a long time I've seen a Jet ski or a water skier—something or someone more my size.

A few people wave at me. I think it's because they see the words "Wisconsin to the Gulf" on my kayak. Seeing all this activity, I realize I haven't had a significant conversation with anyone yet today. Sometimes I feel the loneliest when I'm surrounded by a lot of people. They've probably come a short distance to play in the water. Soon it will be dark and they will return that short distance back home to their families. I, on the other hand, will be alone. Today is the first time on this trip that I feel like it's been a long time since I've been home.

Sometimes I feel like I'm progressing slowly. I would really like to catch some faster current, but under these low-water conditions, I'm not sure if it's possible. A fifty-mile day, that's what I long for. Well, dreaming about it isn't going to get me anywhere, so I keep paddling for another hour and a half.

I am hot and tired. It's time to look for a stopping place. There are several boats scattered among the sandbars. I find a low sandbar next to a rock dike and a section of woods, where I can be by myself.

After setting up camp, I cook supper. It seems my food supply is hardly dwindling. I also still have three quarts of fuel. I was hoping to lessen the weight of my kayak by using up more supplies. I start a small fire and burn one quart of fuel. I hope I won't regret this later.

Before retiring, I check on my kayak. Earlier, I tied it to a two-foot long rock. I stack more rocks on top of the rock anchor. I am confident this will keep my kayak secure throughout the night.

Day 20

N. 38° 57' 51"
W. 90° 40' 42"

As I stated earlier, the best sandy campsites are located just beyond the dams. This is also the best place to experience fluctuations in the water level. Water was released from Lock and Dam 25 raising the water level two feet. I awake at 1:30 a.m. to the sound of my kayak rocking side to side. The wake of a passing barge causes my floating kayak to slosh methodically against the shore. I secure my craft two feet higher up shore, checking it periodically through the night.

Distant thunder and lightning in the northern sky arouses me at 4:45 a.m. Thinking it best to get up now before the rain reaches my camp, I pack everything away in the kayak. In the darkness, paddling by headlamp, I cautiously pick my way along the Missouri shore.

On a sandbar ahead, a small yellow flame flickers from the remnants of a campfire. Two tents are pitched one hundred feet from the dying coals. *Will the occupants hear the storm coming or will they be caught taking down camp in the rain?*

The storm has more bark than bite. The booming thunder and piercing lightning are an elaborate fanfare for a five-minute gentle rain that parades across the sky behind me. Thankful that the storm doesn't amount to much, I sing, hum and whistle old tunes that come to mind.

My eyes strain in the pre-dawn darkness to pick out a lighted channel marker. I like to establish my starting milepost as soon as I start out in the morning, especially when the river winds its way through the country. I can get my daily mileage from the GPS, if I leave it on all day, but to spare batteries, I only turn it on occasionally. Therefore, when I stop at the end of the day, the GPS gives me only a straight-line mileage reading. This means it calculates my mileage from starting point A to ending point B in a straight line, not taking into account the many twists and turns in the river. Because of this, I calculate river mileage using mile markers posted at various points along the river. In Prescott, where I started, the mile marker reads 811.5. This is how many miles between Prescott, Wisconsin, and Cairo, Illinois, located at the southernmost tip of Illinois. From there the mile markers start over again at 958 until the Head of Passes, the end of the Mississippi River in Louisiana. Mile markers give me a precise measurement of how many *river* miles I've conquered throughout the day. As the river widens, I sometimes have a hard time seeing mile markers posted on shore even with ten-power binoculars. On these days, I use other educated guesses to determine the distance I've paddled. If it took me three hours to paddle fifteen miles yesterday, I gauge today's distance similar to yesterday's determination. Also, I can calculate mileage by measurements on my maps.

The sun, rising strong and bright, is a picture of the self-sufficiency I feel this morning. Even though I'm alone on the river, I have everything I need to survive and then some. However, I don't let this feeling of security linger too long in my mind.

Ironic is this self-sufficiency of mine. Yes, I take care of myself day after day on this sometimes unforgiving river, yet modern technology surrounds me. Take for instance, my kayak. Its sleek lines enable me to cut through the wind and water with ease. The virtual weightlessness of my paddle allows my arms to lift it thousands of time a day without exhausting me. My paddle is efficient at pushing tons of water, propelling me toward my goal. The GPS guides me and pinpoints my location at every turn in the river. The VHS marine radio informs me of potential threatening weather, so I am not caught unaware. It also keeps my in contact with the locks and large commercial vessels. This list could go on and on. So you see, even though it appears to me at times that I am living on the edge by my own power and knowledge, ironically I'm also dependent upon the technology around me. I will have many people to thank when I complete this journey.

At mid-morning, as I am peacefully admiring the rocky bluffs lining the riverbank, I am startled by gunshots. Using my binoculars to investigate, I witness two people, one much taller than the other, dressed in camouflage; one is carrying a rifle. I approach cautiously. "Is it hunting season?" I question.

"Yeah, squirrel season," the man replies.

"It's good to see fathers and sons spending time together," I comment.

"People wonder why we have so much trouble with kids these days," the man begins. "Most parents don't spend time with their kids—good time and lots of it. My boy and I spend a lot of time hunting and fishing together," he continues.

Seemingly bored, the bright-eyed and energetic nine-year-old skips old clamshells across the water. He makes me think of Isaac. *How's he getting along in school? How's his football season going? I wish he could be on this trip with me.*

As everyone seems to do, the father warns me about the dangers of the river below St. Louis. Thanking him for the warning, I paddle on, leaving them to their hunting.

. I paddle three more hours. Needing to stretch my legs, I aim for a small, sand spit. As I am about to land, a snake's head pokes out of the river, then another and another—15 snakes in all! Deciding that maybe this isn't the best place to stop, I get out of there doing the snake paddle. The snake paddle, as I call it, is a shallow stroke, keeping the blades of my paddle low, so as not to scoop up any snakes and have them slide down my paddle shaft onto me. This brief episode gives me the extra adrenaline I need to keep going.

Because I now have to keep paddling, I am grateful that the wind is out of the north-northwest. Although the wind is creating waves, they aren't causing any problems for me yet.

I angle toward the east side keeping an eye open for a landing spot. It isn't long before I find myself near Alton, Illinois. I shift in my seat and flex my leg muscles. Beyond two colorful gambling boats anchored near shore, a small docking area catches my eye. Large, expensive-looking yachts rock in the wavy waters of the marina. *I hope no one thinks I'm riff raff.* Stiffly, I exit the kayak and walk with a slight hobble to a pop machine, where I purchase a couple of bottles of Mt. Dew. I pace back and forth on the dock while drinking one pop. I pack the other pop away and slip into my faithful Gulfstream. I paddle under the Alton Bridge making my way to the channel.

If my calculations are correct, I've paddled between thirty and thirty-five miles so far today. During my short break at the marina, the wind increased fifteen to twenty miles per hour creating three-foot following seas (waves that come from behind). For these reasons and because I'm tired, I will look for a camping location as soon as I pass through Lock and Dam 26, two miles away.

A quarter-mile from the dam, I radio the lockmaster, requesting southbound passage. A tow will soon be exiting the lock, putting me next in line. Within the next ten minutes, the wind's strength increases piling the water up into four-foot waves near the lock walls. If conditions were calm, I would hang onto a rung of the ladder recessed in the long wall, providing an opportunity for me to rest before my turn. Four-foot waves are smashing into the gates and ricocheting back at me, causing confused seas. I am weary from paddling backwards to maintain my position and to keep from being slammed into the lock gates.

Earlier, the day had been warm, so I removed my shirt, wearing only my life jacket. Now, with the air temperature dropping, the wind howling and the waves breaking over the back deck of my boat soaking me, my body temperature is cooling rapidly. These elements mixed with exhaustion set the stage for hypothermia. I am well versed in the signs of hypothermia, so I monitor my declining condition. *Am I shivering? Are my thought processes clear?*

I have been struggling for forty minutes with no word from the lock. *What is taking so long? I don't know how much longer I can hold on!* With the dam on the right and jagged rocks on the left, I have no place to rest. I battle the waves to reach my radio. I am glad I invested the extra money in a submersible VHF marine radio, because it is getting thoroughly soaked. I call the lock again to see what's the holdup. "Lock and Dam 26, this is Kayaker. How much more time will it be before I can lock through? I don't know how long I can hold out!" The wind and waves thrust me forward. I drop the radio—tethered to my life jacket—onto my spray skirt in front of me. Wearily, I back paddle, attempting to regain the distance I lost. Bracing with my paddle, I struggle to maintain balance in my kayak.

"Where are you Kayaker? I can't see you," the lockmaster responds.

I quickly grab my radio. "I'm by the long wall. Do you see me now?"

"I can hardly hear you," he responds. "I'm filling the chamber for you now. It will only take about three minutes."

Fifteen seconds later a worker comes to the long wall. From the safety of the cement wall, he watches me bob up and down. "You're doing a good job!" he encourages. "The wind came up fast and real strong," he yells over the wind. "Even the barges get blown over to the side in winds like these."

"When the gates start to open, move toward them slowly," he instructs. I watch the wind blow the tops off the waves and into the lock chamber. The gate opens; two boats exit. Their wakes produce reflection waves that slop up and down and swish side-to-side, bouncing back and forth between the cement wall and the boats. The waves toss me about like a small twig thrown into relentless, turbulent waters. Slowly I inch forward. The worker walks along the cement wall, following me into the lock chamber. "We get real nervous when small boats like yours are in wind like this."

"Thanks for coming out," I say, comforted by his presence. There is no relief, as the wind causes havoc with the water inside the lock as well. There are no ropes to hold onto, so I continue to brace and back paddle as the water is released from the chamber.

The worker informs me there is a barge ready to enter from the south. "When you leave the lock, go to your starboard side." The lock gates open. The waiting barge is much closer than I had anticipated. The swirling waters jerk at my steadfast kayak. I maneuver my craft to the right as instructed.

Finally free of the lock, I move down the river, sapped of nearly all my energy. I need to find a campsite quickly. My maps indicate an island a half-mile down river. I set up camp and eat a quick supper on its sandbar protected from the murderous winds. I anticipate reaching St. Louis, Missouri, tomorrow, so I muster up enough strength to shave and wash clothes. I flop into the tent and fall asleep to the sound of wind seething through the treetops.

Day 21

N. 38° 51' 45"
W. 90° 08' 59"

I wake to the same some sound that I slept through all night—the howling wind. The north-northwest winds seem to be waging war high up in the skies against the southern breezes that dominated the atmosphere of my journey this far.

I still feel drained. Since I left Prescott three weeks ago, I have not taken a day off from paddling. After yesterday's bout with the wind and waves, I'm thinking it might be a good day to rest and reorganize my gear. If I paddle today, I will face the Chain of Rocks (a natural rock rapids) and the potentially heavy boat and barge traffic of St. Louis . I prefer to face these things feeling strong, physically and mentally.

The northwest winds bring cooler temperatures—about twenty degrees cooler. The warmer the weather the more I sweat and the more water I consume. I don't mind cool weather.

Even though my decision to take a day off from paddling is wise, for me, staying in one spot is like leaving a running car sit in the driveway. It uses up gasoline, but goes nowhere. My body is resting, but I still need food and water. I'm using up my resources, but not eating up river miles. This is why I like to have at least two-day's water supply with me at all times. If I injure myself or have problems with my kayak or, like today, need a rest from a tiring day's paddle, I will always have a cushion of rations to depend on until I am able to continue on.

Since I'm not in a hurry this morning, a breakfast of scrambled eggs sounds delicious. I garnish them with ketchup from fast-food restaurant packets I smuggled along. *I'm living on the wild side now!*

After breakfast I wash the clothing that I've worn several days in a row, such as my vest and a pair of pants or two. In a short time they are dry—thanks to the wind—and I am able to fold and pack them away in dry bags. I re-fold some of my clean clothes to conserve space. I also re-evaluate the necessity of my gear. If I use something often during the day, I transfer it to a more accessible location, such as the deck bag. If I use something less often than I had anticipated, I bury it deeper in the kayak. I find my temperature gauge that has eluded me for a couple of weeks. At 9:30 a.m. it is fifty-four degrees.

Preparing an elaborate breakfast, doing the laundry and reorganizing my provisions are exhausting work. It's time for a nap. Sleeping soundly for an hour and a half, confirms my decision to stay put today is a wise one.

In mid-afternoon, as I'm in my tent reading the book Gordy gave me, I hear a helicopter in the distance. It approaches, and soon it is hovering above my campsite. I observe the helicopter's movements through a small, plastic window in the rain fly. It circles slowly, taking one last look, before leaving. Because of the terrorist attacks on 9-11, they must have been suspicious of the half-mile proximity of my camp in relation to the lock and dam. I return to my reading, but soon I'm overcome with drowsiness.

Feeling refreshed from my second nap of the day, I walk about the island exercising my legs. During my scouting adventure, a large hawk swoops down into the backwaters, snatching up a catfish in its sharp talons. The hawk struggles to lift the fish above the surface of the water. With wings flapping slowly and tips touching the water, the hawk reaches shore. Just as it begins to enjoy the fruits of its labor, a murder of crows appears. They hover in close, flapping and pecking the hawk. The hawk is able to rip off a few bits of fish before it tries to go airborne, the heavy fish still flopping. Straining, the hawk reaches the branch of a tree, but the crows are right behind. No longer able to protect its prey, the hawk drops the fish and flies off. The crows score one; the hawk, zero.

Before night falls, I scan my maps, planning tomorrow's path through St. Louis. The greatest decision I face is whether to choose the longer, slower and safer route through the canal or go through the Chain of Rocks, which is shorter, faster and potentially more dangerous. Unsure at this point, I will wait until I reach the fork in the river before making my final decision.

As the sun sinks below the horizon, anxious feelings about tomorrow's uncertainties arise. *How congested will the boat traffic be? Will the river be as swift and as dangerous as I've been warned about? Which route will I take through St. Louis? Will I be able to fill up with water before leaving St. Louis? Will I be able to find campsites after the last lock and dam?*

I don't know why I always worry about things— especially water and campsites. I am reminded of the Bible passage in St. Matthew, where the Lord Jesus says, "…I tell you, do not worry about your life, what you will eat or drink; or about your body, what you will wear… Look at the birds of the air; they do not sow or reap or store away in barns, and yet your heavenly Father feeds them…. Who of you by worrying can add a single hour to his life?" I take heart in this passage; it erases my anxious feelings.

Burrowed into my sleeping bag, I lay still, listening. It is very quiet; the wind has calmed. I fall asleep to the sounds of silence and the images of the St. Louis Arch.

Day 22

N. 38° 51' 45"
W. 90° 08' 59"

After a full day's rest, I am up early, eager to fall into my normal regimen. Paddling begins at 6:25 a.m.; I want to get an early jump on the St. Louis area.

But even before I reach St. Louis, I must contend with the Missouri River entering the Mississippi. *I wonder if it will change the Mississippi in any way. Will I have nasty currents to deal with as these two giants collide, each fighting for their rightful place?* Within minutes, I approach the confluence—all seems fine. I sneak a peek up the Missouri River. It appears small to me, more so than I had anticipated. Also the water is much muddier in color. A raised line of water, a hundred yards in length, forms downstream from where the two rivers converge. It gives me the impression that the Missouri and the Mississippi Rivers are working together, rather than battling against each other.

The wind is calm and the tow traffic is light—only three tows in the first two hours. I strain my eyes to the skyline trying to catch a glimpse of the tall, silver gateway arch near the waterfront of St. Louis. It still eludes me.

I reach the point in the river where I must decide to go left through the canal, or straight ahead through the Chain of Rocks. On the shore a large sign reads, "ALL BOATS USE THE CANAL." I am not thrilled about paddling through an eight-mile canal empty of current, but full of barges. I've read of and talked to paddlers who have successfully navigated the Chain of Rocks. Straight ahead it is.

Two miles after passing the canal opening, I experience a stark sense of isolation. There are no other boats around and no sights or sounds of human or city life.

I feel my kayak picking up speed as if it is being funneled into something. Focusing intently on the river, I catch glimpses of white flashes on the water's surface, a third of a mile ahead. I knew this to be a sign of rapids. With the force of the water increasing still more, I paddle to the Missouri side in case I need to make a quick exit. The flickers grow larger, and the water swifter. I pull up close to shore and proceed cautiously. I approach the Chain of Rocks as close as I feel safe.

Because I sit very low in the water, it is difficult to see what lies before me. Finding a convenient landing spot, I get out to survey the rapids. *I may be able to run them in my sea kayak, but I am not going to do something stupid to end my trip now after making it almost to St. Louis.*

In thirty minutes, I take everything out of the kayak and carefully portage around the first fifty yards of the rock chain—the riskiest section to paddle through. I load everything back into the kayak and cover the cockpit to prevent water from filling the boat.

I begin lining (the process of holding onto a rope that is tied to both ends of the kayak, then walking along the shore guiding the kayak as it floats through the rapids) my kayak through the next 150 yards or so. Holding the paddle and the rope together in both hands, I steer the kayak around rocks and logs. All is progressing well until I come to a huge culvert, belching dirty water.

On my right, the culvert protrudes from a bank too steep to climb. In front of me lay a log resting on a ledge and submerged one to two inches below the water's surface. To the left of the log, the water looks to be five feet deep. The only way for me to cross, is to jump to the log, walk the length of it to the other end, then jump to land on the other side. I untie the rope from the stern, leaving it tied to the bow. Holding the loose end of the rope in one hand and my paddle in the other, I leap, my right foot stretching for the submerged log. My muddy shoe splashes through the silty waters, finding its mark. Gripping the log, I hold my footing. Taking two or three quick steps, I hurdle to solid ground beyond the culvert opening. My kayak had floated ahead of me, but now waits patiently for me like a loyal dog waits for his master—always ready and willing.

All that remains of the rapids is a few scattered rocks. Confident I can paddle safely through this last section, I stow my rope and climb back into the cockpit of my kayak. Pushing off, I excitedly search the horizon for the towering arch, marking the presence of St. Louis, Missouri.

Taking a deep breath, I paddle forward. There are no other boats here yet, so the river is all mine. Shortly, though, a small Coast Guard boat flies up the river toward me. Thinking it is coming to reprimand me, I am relieved when it buzzes past me, as if I'm not even here.

It isn't long before the boat channel re-enters the river, bringing with it several colossal barges. With tense muscles and heightened senses, I weave in and out of commercial boat traffic passing Mosenthein Island. There it stands, just beyond Merchants Bridge, majestic and beautiful, the Gateway Arch of St. Louis. I had dreamed many nights of this moment. While still afloat, I snap three photos of this awe-inspiring monument. My eyes follow one column down to earth. A rickety, wooden shack stands along the river wall. On the wall is spray painted, "I'm not alone. Jesus lives with me." My focus returns to what is truly awesome: I am not alone on this river; God is with me. With the number of commercial vessels tripling, I watch very closely, anticipating their every move. Most of the danger is near the sides of the river, so I stay close to the main channel where traffic seems to flow in an orderly fashion. Sometimes I hurry forward and other times I hold up, letting a tow pass in front. At the same time, my eyes scan the riverfront for a convenient place to land and find water.

For some, being surrounded by people and buildings is security and protection. For me, I am comfortable with solitude. Even though I'm not able to replenish my dwindling water supply, I happily leave the hustle and bustle of St. Louis behind, looking forward to peace and quiet.

I relax into a constant paddling rhythm, as the number of barges diminishes. Turning my attention to the important issue of drinking water, I search the west bank. I brought along water purification tablets and a water filter pump, with the intent of using them in an emergency—I don't feel this is an emergency situation. Now ten miles south of St. Louis, my eyes fall on a floating dock. I join the few boats tied up at Hoppies Marina. The current is fairly swift here, so I exit my kayak carefully. All is still and no voices can be heard. I grab my water bags and begin my search. "Is anyone here?" I yell. I call two more times with no response.

Finding a water hose, I turn the valve releasing clear water. After filling my water bags, I put the hose back exactly how I found it. Returning my water containers to the kayak, I wonder if the phone booth on the floating dock works. Putting the receiver to my ear, I am surprised to hear a dial tone. Using a calling card, I make a call to my wife, a middle school secretary. My son is in a classroom nearby, so I am able to speak with him as well. It is encouraging to hear his voice. It sounds deeper than when I left. Soon it is time to say, "Good-bye."

Returning the receiver to its hook, I look around—still no one. "Thank you, Hoppies," I say softly, as I make my way back to the kayak. I slip into the kayak and paddle on, eager to find out how *different* the Mississippi River is below St. Louis.

At 4:30 p.m. I find a secluded sandbar—its sand so pure and white, it almost seems artificial. I pull my kayak on shore and have a look around. No sign of humans whatsoever; only animal tracks litter this pristine beach.

As usual, I cook supper and set up camp. After hanging a few damp articles of clothing, I take a walk to exercise my lower body. Returning to camp, I recall the changes of the river I've witnessed since leaving St. Louis.

On the upper section, I truly felt as though I was paddling the Mississippi River. Now, several miles below St. Louis, I feel as though I've been transported to a remote river in a faraway land. The river traffic has dwindled to practically nothing; I haven't seen a town since I left St. Louis; and there are no grain elevators or power plants to speak of. Fewer islands dot the river; and the shorelines, once crowded with dense vegetation, are now more open, making it easier to view wildlife. I've spotted turkeys and deer several times today. The river's current has increased some—maybe two or three miles per hour. Because of the added waters of the Missouri River, the Mississippi is wider. There are no more locks and dams to create large pools. The river, in some ways, is set free, guided only by wing dams and dikes that keep it in check. Our society is much the same; we are a free country, guided by rules and laws that keep us in check.

I sit near the water, soaking up the last few rays of sunlight. Only the chirps of birds and the occasional howl of a coyote break the silence. The river mixing and turning as it flows swiftly past mesmerizes me. I feel comfortable with the new changes.

As evening loosens its grip, I ease into my sleeping bag. A coyote howls—the last thing I remember before slipping off to sleep.

Day 23

N. 38° 11' 49"
W. 90° 20' 05"

I wake to the same sound I fell asleep to—a coyote's howl. I crawl from my tent and stretch, eager to experience what the day has in store for me—more beauty, more sandbars and more remoteness. The sun is beginning its job of warming my world to a comfortable seventy degrees—a perfect paddling temperature.

The desire to paddle fifty miles today is so incredibly strong; I scramble to take down camp. I gently glide my kayak into the tranquil river. Even though the surface of the water is calm, I can feel the power in its steady progress. The Mississippi has an air of confidence; it knows where it is going and is eager to get there. Like the river, I'm headed to the Gulf, fifty miles at a time, hopefully.

I paddle at a constant pace, with few distractions. In the early hours I notice deer on the riverbank, and later, a coyote scouring a sandbar looking for anything edible or interesting. A couple of barges and three or four yachts come into distant view and then disappear. No fishermen, that I can see, cast nets or lines. I converse with no one today.

I make camp on a sandy shore of Illinois, fifty-three miles from last night's site. I am tired—not the tiredness felt after a stressful day at work, but an exhilarating exhaustion after a successful workout. I am relieved that I am able to finally break the fifty-mile mark. I am full of anticipation—eager to do it again. What an incredible way to end the day.

Day 24

N. 37° 42' 57"
W. 89° 35' 10"

My maps and GPS indicate I am about twenty-nine miles from Cape Girardeau, Missouri. The morning air is thick, and heavy dew may saturate the rain fly of my tent, but my desire to reach Cape Girardeau is not dampened. I can hear you ask, "I thought you liked solitude, seclusion? Why are you so eager to get to a big town? I thought you didn't care for cities?"

Of course, I hope to replenish my water supply. More importantly, I hope to meet a couple that once lived in Prescott, Wisconsin. My wife works with Eileen at Prescott Middle School. She and her husband Ed are friends with Mike and Kathy who now live in Cape Girardeau. I have their phone number and plan to call them when I reach town. I am a little apprehensive to impose myself on someone I do not know, especially after the disappointing meeting in southern Wisconsin, but I will give it a try.

I push away from my campsite in the darkness. I listen carefully for any sounds of danger. All I can hear is the gentle stroke of the paddle as it enters and exits the water. The river seems to be all mine again; it has been since leaving St. Louis.

At 9:30 am the sun carves its way through the blanket of dense fog, revealing that I am no longer alone on the river. Barges and yachts begin crowding into my territory. Cape Girardeau must be close.

An hour after midday, I spy a man eating his lunch while seated on a small, wooden boat dock outside Cape Girardeau city limits. I paddle over to the man. "Good day," I greet, my voice squeaking from not being used for two days.

"Hi, there," he responds.

"Do you know of a boat launch up ahead?"

"Well, there's a spot up there, but I'm not sure if you can get to it with that vacation barge in the way."

"Do you know if there's a gas station or another place close by where I can use a phone?"

"The closest gas station is about two to three miles from here. Nothing close. Then again I'm not from here. I just work in town." The man in his early forties, wearing a mechanics shirt—the kind with a name patch—goes back to eating his lunch.

I thank him for what little information he is able to give me and continue down along the waterfront of Cape Girardeau. I paddle to within fifteen feet of the enormous vacation barge (a barge renovated into a pleasure craft). Several passengers, seated at tables, wave to me from behind large, tinted glass windows. I naturally wave back. Circling the floating hotel, I find a narrow passage between it and the rock shore. Careful not to bang my kayak against the rocks, I manage my way out of the cockpit. I secure the kayak to a rock. I am uncomfortable with this arrangement; the barge could crush my boat without knowing it. Looking up, I make eye contact with the captain. "You won't squish me, will you Captain?" I yell up to him.

"I'll take off slow and easy. You'll be okay," he assures me. "You should wear a coffee can on your head, though," he says. "My radar doesn't pick you up, otherwise. You're too low to the water and don't have any metal to reflect my radar."

"Thanks," I respond. "I'll keep that in mind." I am glad that I now know that a barge's radar can't detect me; I will need to be extremely cautious. One could run me down without realizing it.

The riverboat barge departed at 2:15 p.m. Kneeling next to my kayak, I watch to make sure the wheel wash doesn't cause my kayak to bang against the rugged rock shore. The captain is gracious, guiding his boat away with the smallest wake. With that obstacle gone, I line my kayak along the shoreline to a small gravel spot, about the size of my kayak. Gently I pull my boat ashore. As I am tying it down, a man approaches. "Another barge will be tying up here shortly."

"Should I move my kayak?" I ask.

"No. You'll be okay here." Don, also a kayaker, asks, "Do you need anything?"

"I was wondering if you could *show me* where I can get some water and a place to make a local phone call?"

Small craft parking is a bit challenging at the Cape Girardeau waterfront.

With water bags and a small fanny pack in tow, I follow Don to the Cape Restaurant. He leads me through the back door into the kitchen, assisting me in filling my water bags. He then offers me a business phone to make my call. Don's help goes above and beyond what I had anticipated; I am very grateful.

I'm a little anxious about making a phone call to people I have never met. Thinking the worst they can say is, "Get lost, River Rat," I dial the number and wait. It rings—once, twice, three times. Thinking no one is home, I begin to return the receiver back to its cradle. Then I hear a lady's voice say, "Hello?"

"Hi, is this Kathy?"

"Yes?" she replies.

"I'm Byron Curtis from Prescott, Wisconsin—the kayaker paddling to the Gulf."

"Oh, yes, Ed and Eileen said you might be coming down the river. What time did you get into town?" she asks.

"About one o'clock."

Then she says the magic words, "Do you need anything?"

Even though I don't actually need much, her words are music to my ears. "Would it be possible for you to take me to a grocery store?"

She is willing and asks me for my location. I describe my surroundings and she says that she will meet me in thirty minutes. Before hanging up, I thank her and tell her how much I appreciate the kind gesture. *I hope I don't smell too badly.*

As I leave the restaurant to prepare for my rendezvous, a man approaches me and asks, "Are you the kayaker?"

"Yes?"

"Well, a local television reporter is looking for you."

"They are?"

"If you wait here a few minutes, they should be back."

Within five minutes, a black SUV pulls up and two men get out.

"Are you the kayaker?" ask the one with the tie and dress shirt.

"Yes, I'm the kayaker."

"I'd like to interview you."

Agreeing to the reporter's proposition, I lead both men down to the waterfront to where my kayak waits patiently. For nearly a half hour, the man in jeans videotapes as I describe my trip and show them my craft and gear. The reporter interjects questions from time to time. At the end of the interview, I ask if I can take a picture of them.

"No one has ever asked to take *our* picture." Both men grin for my camera.

As the cameraman and reporter are packing up their equipment, I notice a lady walking my way. She glances from person to person as if looking for someone in particular.

"Are you Kathy?" I ask.

"You must be Byron," she says with a smile.

With much persuasion, I snap a couple of pictures of Kathy in front of the Cape Girardeau sign, before leaving the waterfront with her. She helps me load a few of my items into her Ford Explorer, but I have to leave my kayak where it is. *I hope it and all my gear will be waiting for me when I return.*

As Kathy is shuttling me to a grocery store, she offers me room and board for the night. My mouth waters at the thought of eating a real meal. *Maybe I can take a shower—my first in three weeks.* Needless to say, I accept Kathy's offer.

Upon entering the store, my eyes dart from row to row, overwhelmed by the endless selection of food. My stomach churns; for some reason, I don't want any of it—maybe it's because I haven't had variety in several weeks. To be gracious to my host, I choose a 2 ½-pound bag of trail mix and four bottles of PowerAde for emergency drinking rations, in case water becomes difficult to find.

After making my purchases, Kathy weaves the Explorer through town to her home. With my bag in hand, I follow Kathy up to the second level of the house where she shows me the bedroom I will be staying in. To the right and at the end of the hall is the bathroom, which is my first priority. I want to let the hot water fall on me for hours. At the same time, I don't want to take advantage of my hostess, so I cut my shower time down to a few minutes. I also spruce up my appearance with a shave and clean clothes before heading back down to the main level.

Kathy offers the use of her washing machine to launder a load of my dirty clothing. While waiting for my clothing, which is getting a real cleaning, Kathy calls her husband, Mike, arranging for us to meet him at the river on his way home from work. He will use his pickup truck to carry my kayak to the house. I am glad I don't have to leave it unattended all night. Because most of my clothes are made of synthetic fibers, they need only a few minutes in the dryer. After my clothes are folded and returned to the dry bag, Kathy and I make our way back to my kayak—hopefully it is still where I left it.

Mike and the kayak are waiting for us when we arrive. Together, Mike and I angle my boat into the bed of the truck, half of it hanging beyond the tailgate. Using rope, we tie it securely to keep it in the truck during transport. Once back at the house, Mike pulls the truck into the garage, leaving the kayak in place, ready for the return trip to the river in the morning.

Mike, once a tow captain and still in the "tow biz," as he says, studies his Army Corps of Engineers maps with me. He is a wealth of information, pointing out places to find water, dangerous areas to stay away from and secluded locations to camp. He also gives me a few hints about towboats. His expertise renews the adventurous spirit in me.

It has been about seven hours since I had anything to eat, so my saliva glands water as they talk about supper. They treat me to a delicious steak and all the trimmings at the Outback Steak House. I'm not able to finish the entire meal, since lately I'm not accustomed to eating so much in one sitting. *But boy, was it good!*

Once back at their place, we talk for a bit and they offer me the use of their cell phone to call home. I am able to catch up on all that has happened with Wendi and Isaac, as well as bring them up to speed on my progress. Isaac has been having some great football games and actually scored the first points of the season for his team. That makes a dad proud. Even though we are able to talk for a fair amount of time, the phone call ends all too quickly, as we say our good-byes once again.

I manage to stay awake for the ten o'clock news, where I catch a glimpse of the television interview I had earlier today. Kathy videotapes it for me as a souvenir. It is awkward watching myself on TV, and in front of others.

I had quite a busy day and am pretty tired by this time, so I excuse myself to the bedroom. I undress and stand naked in front of a large, dresser mirror. For the first time in several weeks, I am able to see the impact of my journey on my body. Lifting and curling my arms, my triceps and biceps bulge, while ribs show themselves more predominately. I calculate I have lost close to twelve pounds. Turning to look at my back, I see more muscle definition—paddling 1,000 strokes each mile has a way of strengthening the upper body. I also see signs of weariness—tan and weathered skin and tired eyes. Sometimes, we as individuals can feel confident and strong. We think we can take on the world—attack any obstacle and confront any fear. Yet the smallest, microscopic virus or bacteria that can turn us into whimpering and whining fools begging for relief can afflict us. The slightest mistake or miscalculation can cause injury or even death. I would never claim to be the best paddler or the best at anything, for that matter. I know that life is a fragile walk and as sure as I can be victorious, I can also be a failure. I am thankful for each day. The time spent in front of the mirror is only a few seconds, yet its reflection reveals volumes of my 39 years of life.

Giving into feelings of exhaustion and the invitation of a comfortable bed, I slip between the sheets. With eyes closed, I doze to images of drifting effortlessly on billowy clouds, sneaking a bird's-eye peak of the Mississippi winding below me.

Day 25

N. 37° 18' 18"

W. 89° 31' 02"

The night quickly gives way into morning. After breakfast, Mike delivers my kayak and me to the river on his way to work. Shaking hands, I thank him for allowing me, a stranger, into his home. Quickly, we depart. As I pass under the bridge, Mike honks his horn and I wave. I hope I will see Mike and Kathy again someday.

I am recharged as I leave Cape Girardeau. With a good night's rest in a comfortable bed, my water supply replenished, and useful information from an experienced tow captain, I have renewed enthusiasm to continue my journey from bluffs to bayous.

The landscape of the countryside is changing. In southern Wisconsin and Minnesota I was surrounded by stately bluffs, home to majestic bald eagles. Farmlands met the riverbanks in Iowa and central Illinois. Now that I am near the tip of southern Illinois, soon to pass into Kentucky, the occasional bluff greets me once again.

Soon the Ohio River, which defines the state line between Illinois and Kentucky, will join the Mississippi. Mike says to expect the river to widen after the merge. This should allow plenty of room for me to stay clear of commercial traffic. This also means crossings will be long and will take away from my southward progress. An increase in current speed looks promising. What I am anticipating is an incredible display of power when these two massive rivers collide.

The afternoon brings a strong southeasterly wind forcing me to the Illinois side. Instead of being sucked into the river's turbulent middle, I switch to the Missouri side, hugging the outside edge where the rivers merge.

I paddle hard, wanting to put the long anticipated union behind me. The closer I get to the junction, the more the barge traffic increases. This doesn't worry me; rather, it causes me to be more observant in my navigation.

True to my plan, I stay near the west bank. I pass under the bridge that crosses the Mississippi, connecting Cairo, Illinois, to the state of Missouri. Surprisingly, the river's edge becomes shallow and the banks are muddy. I paddle out, not far, but just beyond the submerged, mucky ledge to deeper water. I look across, where the two rivers become one, expecting to see choppy waters, swirling whirlpools and standing waves. Instead, the rivers seem to gently weave themselves together into one fluid path.

It is 5:00 p.m. and I am exhausted from paddling fifty-five miles today. *I just want to find a place to lay my tired body.* Looking to my left, my eyes, for some reason, rise to where a large, white cross, reflecting the evening sunlight, stands high atop a bluff near Wyckliffe, Kentucky. *There's got to be a campsite at the foot of the cross.* Observing a break in the dozen barges moving up and down the Kentucky side of the river, I make a quick and decisive decision to sprint for the eastern shore. Pointing my kayak toward the cross, I soon discover that the fast-moving current will force me beyond my intended target. I change the angle of my approach to a point upstream from the cross. Because the river is unexpectedly narrow (which is why the current is swift), I reach the opposite shore in ten minutes. *Just as I believed, a safe haven awaits me.* A small sandy area rests, protected from the wind by a towering bluff to the east.

I scoot my kayak on shore and tie it to a huge beached log. Up the sloping bank, nestled in the trees, is a flat area, perfect for my tent. I quickly complete my routine camp chores.

Sadly enough, I eat the last of my bite-sized Snickers bars that a coworker had given me. I have become accustomed to devouring a small morsel of chocolate at the end of the day; now they are gone.

An achy back tells me I've paddled enough today. My lips are cracked and sore; I forgot to put sunscreen on them today. If I smile too wide, they bleed. I'll have to refrain from telling jokes to myself tonight. "Ha, ha, ha! Ouch!"

I rest easy in my serene camp this evening, reading from my small Bible, and the book Gordy gave me. I listen to the weather forecast before falling asleep.

Day 26

N. 36° 57' 26"
W. 89° 05' 42"

I get a late start this morning. The daylight hours are shrinking; the sun is sleeping in more, lately.

With the lack of rain, the water level is low. The Mississippi has retreated from the wide territory it once ruled, leaving behind enormous sandbars, some the size of mini-deserts. Surprisingly, the current is spotty; at times it is strong, at other times it seems to be barely moving. The river mile markers are not giving up their miles as quickly today. I am frustrated because I have conquered at least fifty miles each of the last two days and would like to keep this pace.

Late morning, I leave the channel. Hoping to save time, I take a shortcut around the left side of the Middle Bar island.

According to my map, this route is a straight shot. After paddling for several minutes, my eyes squint, capturing glimpses of small, quick flashes. *I've seen this before—the Chain of Rocks.* Committed to this path, and not wanting to paddle upstream to return to the main channel, I proceed cautiously. A rock dike emerges ahead. The dike cuts off the Mississippi River between Kentucky and the Middle Bar island, with two 100-yard openings letting water escape. As I had anticipated, the current quickly picks up speed. I sprint for the Kentucky bank, choosing against the right opening; if anything happens to my kayak or me, I don't want to be stranded on an island.

I secure my kayak to the rock dike; *I don't want it drifting away here.* Walking to the end of the rock dike to overlook the left passage route, I am glad I didn't try paddling through it. Water speeds through this narrow corridor, slamming against submerged boulders and flipping back against the current in whitecaps as it drops three feet. The ingenuity of man tries to force the river to go around the other side of the Middle Bar, but the Mississippi revolts and charges through anyway.

Testing the river's strength, I throw a log into the water above the rapids. As the log enters the drop, it instantly shoots ahead, buried by the boiling, turbulent water. I am troubled when the log does not emerge. *I don't want to recreate the same scene with my kayak.* I throw a second test log into a different area, but get the same results. *Well, I guess I won't be paddling through.*

I consider my other options—portage over nasty loose rocks or line the kayak through the very edge of the passage that still grips the two logs I threw in. I stand there for a minute,

This shortcut almost proved to be disastrous.

contemplating and calculating the pros and cons of each choice. Saving portaging for last resorts, I commit to lining the kayak. I tie the ropes together as I did at the Chain of Rocks, checking each knot twice. And like before, I cover the cockpit, in the event it should tip. I snug up my life jacket and place my paddle off to the side, leaving both hands free to manipulate the rope.

Taking in two deep breaths, I gently ease my beautiful, red and white Gulfstream, stern first, into the water's flow; the water would catch the raised bow of the kayak and pull it under if I line it front first. Feeling the tug of the current strengthening, my hands clench the rope, knowing it is the only thing joining me to all my gear and my only means of transportation. Feeling an instant surge of power, I fight to hold fast to my kayak. The force of the water yanks me to the ground, dragging me across the sharp rocks. *Don't let go! Don't let go! Hold on for all you're worth!* The river does not give up its grip and neither do I. But the river seems to be winning, dragging me closer and closer to the swift turbulent waters.

Now the rope is twisted around my left hand and snagged on my watchband. I have to get it untwisted or the river will claim us both. With all my might, I rise up on my knees and give a big jerk on the rope. During the split second that the rope slackens, I rapidly untwist the rope from my wrist. Realizing my weight is not enough to stop the continued beating the river is giving my kayak and me, instantly, I sling the rope around a large rock, hoping together we can conquer the river. The rope holds and the kayak is beyond the rapids, but the force of the water pushes down on the bow of the kayak, elevating the stern. Picking myself up and regaining my footing, slowly I unwrap the rope from around the rock and maneuver my wounded craft to the calm, downstream side of the dike. I secure my kayak and investigate the damage. Two areas of gel coat—the shining outer layer—are chipped off. *I hope it doesn't leak.*

I sit down on a rock to gather my thoughts and slow my rapid breathing. I look back, analyzing the area that I just came through. Feeling weak, I determine that eating is the best thing for me right now.

Reaching for a dry bag in my kayak hatch, I notice blood on my right hand. Two glistening streams of bright red blood make their way down my two middle fingers. I don't feel pain until I see the blood—*isn't that the way it goes?* Wondering if I have any other injuries, I pull up my pant's legs, revealing two scraped shins. The shins are not too bad, so I let the pant's legs down. Right now, I am more concerned about getting infection in the right paddling hand. I clean my wound with drinking water and dab it with Bacitracin antibiotic ointment before covering it with a waterproof bandage. With the first aid applied, I gobble down a couple mouthfuls of trail mix to help replenish the energy I lost in the struggle.

Returning the food bag and first aid kit to the dry hatch, I investigate the damage to my boat more closely. Looks like I slightly cracked the fiberglass behind the skeg and took off a patch of gel coat farther back. *I think she'll still float. I'll paddle for an hour or two and check the rear hatch for any water leakage then.*

I didn't get more than a quarter-mile downstream, when a commercial fisherman, dressed in orange rain bibs, yells, "Did you come through that?"

"Well, yes and no," I answered. "I lined it through."

"I won't even take my power boat through that!"

All I know, I won't be taking any more shortcuts.

I pull over to the shore to visit with Jeff, a Kentuckian, who's cleaning his nets. We shake hands like we are old river pals. We chat about the river and Jeff shows me his fishing nets, which he uses to catch sturgeon for their caviar. He also gives me a peek into his large basket full of sturgeon; he has a few catfish mixed in. Lifting a sturgeon from the hamper, he turns it over and milks the eggs out by running his hand down the fish's belly while gently squeezing. After removing the eggs, he sets the fish free.

I tell Jeff about banging my kayak on the rocks. He asks to take a look at my boat. "I've worked with fiberglass gel coat before," he informs. After examining it, he assures, "The damage isn't too bad. You may want to cover the damaged areas with duct tape. If it starts to leak, there's an auto parts store in Hickman, Kentucky. You can get something there to fix it up."

I paddle away, satisfied that he confirms my previous prognosis of the damage.

The afternoon weather is just as promising—calm southeast winds and plenty of sunshine. Today, I remember to apply sunscreen, minimizing the burns on my arms and face.

Orange and black butterflies flutter past me. *Why do butterflies cross the river? Are the flowers bigger and brighter? Are the plants greener?* It seems like a risky proposition for such a delicate insect. One gust of wind could send it spiraling down to the surface of the water. Sometimes I feel like a butterfly; paddling all alone down this incredible river in a tiny boat is risky business—this morning's incident helped me to realize that.

A campsite fortress with great wind protection.

Two hours have passed; time to check whether or not my kayak is leaking. I pull over to the nearest sandbar and remove the gear from the rear hatch. Dry. Everything is still dry. This is good news. Even so, I cover the damaged areas with duct tape as Jeff recommended. *Maybe, if it holds up, I will rename it underwater tape.* I put a couple layers of tape on and rub over them several times to increase their adhesive power. *I hope the duct tape lasts a day or two, at least.*

The large dikes that help direct the river are beneficial to me in two ways: one, they serve as wind protection; and two they stop the sand from flowing downriver, creating perfect sandy sites for camping. Even though the river is grander and flows with more authority, it has become a place of refuge and protection for me each night.

I prefer to choose large sandbars and, if the weather is favorable, set up camp out in the open. My theory behind this procedure is to be able to see what's coming from all directions. I also figure that if I'm not pretending to hide, others won't bother me. Tonight there are several large sandbars from which to choose a campsite. I paddle into a natural sandy cove. Dragging my kayak up onto the bar, I pitch my tent near the end of one of its peninsulas.

Hungry after another fifty-mile day, I cook rice and add a bullion cube for flavoring. Because the rice needs to cool some, I carry the pot and a spoon with me as I explore the nearby sand dunes. I take a bite here and there as I'm exercising my legs and looking for anything interesting.

After everything's put away for the night, I relax on the edge of the sandbar next to my kayak. With legs outstretched, I lean back on my arms, watching the sun slowly descend and its zigzag reflection widen on the smooth water. It is amazing to me that on this peaceful Saturday evening, there isn't one recreational boater in sight.

Long after the sun dips below the tree line and as the midnight blue sky creeps closer to the ground, a coyote howls, signaling my curfew.

Day 27

N. 36° 28' 34"
W. 89° 26' 40"

I wake from a deep sleep—the kind where you sleep so hard you rarely change positions. My body aches, not just in one place, but all over. My hand that was injured in yesterday's ordeal is only slightly swollen. Even though the best thing for me to do is to get moving and not prolong this motionless state any longer, I lay for a few more fleeting seconds, reflecting on my childhood.

> *My childhood was filled with adventure and no worries. I would run down to the river, looking for new and exciting things—plants, animals, fish, etc. Often, as a boy, my dad would take me to Hamilton Falls, only a few miles from our house. He would tell me hunting and fishing stories, pointing out places in the river where he would swim or catch*

muskies. He would point up the bank indicating how high the waters flooded. My dad was my hero.

I cherished his stories and craved for the day when I could make my own memories and share them with others. I am now experiencing the trip of a lifetime—creating a legacy to pass on to my son.

My watch reads 6:00 a.m. Slowly, my body pulls its achy muscles out of bed and into action. In no time, my kayak is loaded and back in the water. Floating near shore, I check my map, making quick estimations of distances. I hope for another fifty-mile day. At times checking my progress on the map can be depressing. I paddle for several hours, yet hardly even advance, according to the map. *Hey, as long as the weather is good, I should enjoy myself—no worries.*

At 11:30, I approach an interesting area near New Madrid, Missouri, where the river flows northward for seven miles before it makes its way back south. *Talk about going nowhere fast.* This huge twenty-mile curve forms the borders for three states, Missouri, Kentucky and Tennessee.

New Madrid is inviting with its sloping, grassy banks overlooking the river. Simply built homes give it a small-town feel. I want to stop, but I have no reason to, as my water supply is adequate. Besides, stopping will only delay what little progress I seem to be making.

An interesting observation I've made lately is that barges have been passing me in groups of three or more. I'm not sure why this is. When I see one coming, I can expect to see more, shortly thereafter. A few hours later, another group passes.

I make another check on the map; it shows more turns and curves. This information helps me approach these bends on the deep side, avoiding the shallow water on the inside. Boats can sometimes get hung up on sand bars hiding under a few inches of cloudy water.

.As the water snakes its way to the Gulf, it deposits incredibly large amounts of sand. One can get the feeling they are floating through an endless desert. Blowing unchecked over the surface of the sandbars, the wind creates mini-tornadoes or dirt devils. These powerful gusts ambush passers-by with millions of painful needle-like pebbles.

When a storm comes up quickly on the river, there is no place to hide on a sandbar. Since you are the tallest object around, you are a likely target for lightning to strike. For the most part, a sandbar is ideal, offering perfect areas to land and launch, as well as being relatively clean and bug free.

I continue on at a good pace, about five miles per hour, pushing for another fifty-mile day. I press on, conquering my fifth state, Kentucky, one twist after another. These enormous bends not only drain me physically, but mentally as well. My goal is to reach Caruthersville, Missouri, for water before I camp tonight.

The sun rises high and so does the afternoon temperature. I dip my hand in the muddy water. It feels slightly cooler than the air temperature. I wet a bandanna and wash my face, being careful not to get any water into my mouth. Despite the uncomfortable heat, I continue on with a steady rhythm.

As I wipe salty sweat from my head and neck, I see smoke coming from on top the east bank. I drift closer to the shore where an old camp of sorts—tarps and blankets held up by a few rickety boards—comes into view. Smoke from a fire under the makeshift shelter gently drifts out onto the river. All is quiet as I drift by slowly.

The heat of the afternoon sun continues to beat down. I release the spray skirt from around the cockpit letting in cool air. *Ah, this feels good!* Soon something shiny flashes in front of me. My first thought is, "Snake!" I soon discover it's a tiny, silver fish, about five inches long, flopping about inside my cockpit. *What are the chances that a tiny fish, swimming in the largest river in North America, will leap from the water, at just the right time and at just the right angle, and land in my cockpit, only twenty-two inches wide?* I pick him up and snap a picture of my guest—it's been awhile since I've had a visitor. Momentarily, I think about eating him raw—guts and all—but then decide against it. I plop Freddie Fish back into his watery home. If fish could tell stories, he'd have a good one to tell tonight.

Upon taking a GPS reading, I know that Caruthersville is close—maybe three miles away. A half-mile before the town, a pontoon boat navigates upstream. I wave at the eight or nine people aboard. I stop paddling as they motor around behind me. They ask the usual questions, "Where did you come from?" and "Where are you headed?"

To which I give my usual answer, "Wisconsin to the Gulf."

I skip to more important matters. "Is there somewhere I can get water?"

Several agree that I can get water from the gambling boat ahead. Besides the information, they kindly offer me two Cokes. I thank them before continuing my search for water.

I reach the gambling boat at 4:30 p.m., but I'm not thrilled about getting water here. Then I notice a small boat launch made of cement. I manage to gently nudge my kayak up to it and exit my boat. I secure my kayak and retrieve my empty water bags, one from behind the seat and the other two from the day hatch (designed to be reached by the kayaker while sitting in the cockpit). I walk up the sloping cement ramp to a riverside park at the top. There are a few people scattered about the three to five acre park.

I approach two elderly ladies sitting in a car. "Good evening. Will you show me where I can find drinking water?"

"You coming from the river?" the passenger asks.

"Yes, Ma'am…from Prescott, Wisconsin"

"Been through there lots of times," she says. "I used to be a cook on a barge for many years. Nice town, Prescott."

"I think so, too."

Without further hesitation she says, "You can get water at the grain elevator, over there. Other boats do."

Thanking them, I walk a hundred yards to the elevator offices. A man seated in his truck rolls down his window when I approach.

"Good evening, Sir," I say. "Do you work here?"

"Yes?"

"I was wondering if it would be okay if I get some drinking water from that hose over there? I'm paddling down the river and need some water."

He looks me over as I speak. "Well, I don't know how long that water's been in that pipe over there. Why don't you just go on in the office and get some from the hydrant?"

Hydrant? I don't want to put out a fire—I just want a drink. I look toward the building and then back at the man.

"Here," he says, "I'll show you in the office." We go inside the small offices of the elevator business. "There's the hydrant, there," he says, pointing to a water fountain. The kind man helps me fill my water bags. "So where'd you say you're from?" he asks.

"Prescott, Wisconsin. Up by Minneapolis, Minnesota," I respond.

"Oh, I've been to Minneapolis once," he boasts. "They had snowflakes as big as this." His hands form a circle the size of a softball.

As we walk out to the parking area, I thank him for his willingness to help a stranger. Happy to have water, I make my way back to the river.

The air is still calm, like a humid summer's evening in Wisconsin. A middle-aged couple sits on a bench overlooking the river. They seem to be following every move I make. I return my water bags to their designated location; eyes are watching me. *What are they thinking?* I gently place my faithful kayak back into the river. Once again I enter the cockpit smoothly and push off from shore, taking one last look at the couple on the bench. I give a small wave, hoping to change any negative impressions they may have of me. One gives a small wave back.

Upon taking my first paddle strokes, I turn my attention to my next mission—a campsite. Working my way two more miles down the river, I settle on a sandbar looking much like the last. The sun is beginning its usual downward motion. I check my watch—5:30 p.m. Since I paddled a bit later than usual, I'm curious as to how many miles I piled up today. I check my maps, and according to my calculations, I made fifty miles, and then some—fifty-six to be exact—an exciting accomplishment.

I set up camp quickly and put my usual rice supper on the stove to simmer. I look around. Even though it is the last day of September, green foliage is flourishing. Back home, the leaves are painting the hillsides a patchwork of gold, orange and red. Here in my world, it's as if the seasons are standing still.

With supper finished, I stand quietly, gazing upward. A full moon illuminates the clear sky. I walk along the sandbar trying to hold on to the last day of September. I hate to see it go, for it's one of my favorite months. I look up at the moon one last time and wonder if Wendi and Isaac are looking at it also.

I crawl into my tent, easing my weary body into my sleeping bag.

Day 28

N. 36° 09' 45"
W. 89° 36' 14"

I begin paddling my twenty-eighth day at 7:00 a.m. under clear skies and with the promise of sunshine. However, within thirty minutes a thick, heavy fog covers the river valley like a quilt, limiting my view to a kayak's length. As the river widens and visibility diminishes, the probability of getting off course and putting myself in harms way increases dramatically. My inability to wait for greater visibility is more dangerous than the restrictive fog. I don't like pacing on shore, waiting; I choose to press on.

I scrutinize the map. If I follow the shoreline, I will most likely have to paddle in and out around the numerous dikes. This will double my mileage and cut my southward progress in half. Besides, as the water rounds the ends of dikes it forms eddies, whirlpools and shifting currents—dangers all their own. Despite the inconvenience and the added danger, I will advance along the banks, skirting out and around each dike as I come to it.

I proceed cautiously, with only my hearing to guide me. I listen for any hint of danger—the whoosh of water rushing past a buoy marker; the dull drone of a tow pushing several, heavy barges; the rustling of waters forced around a rocky dike. Carefully, I approach the first dike. Moving parallel to the dike, I paddle upstream slightly, keeping my distance from the turbulent waters near the end of the dike. I work my way out and around the rock dam before heading back to shore. *That went well.*

I proceed to the next dike. Like the first, I paddle parallel to the dam and slightly upstream. To my left, I hear water rushing. Suddenly a channel marker comes into view. *I'm farther out than I care to be.* I start for shore. Instantly the end of the dike appears. The heavy current draws me into the dam. It takes four quick and powerful backward strokes just to stop the forward progress of my heavy kayak. *Wow! That was close!* I navigate in and out around each dike for more than three hours, until the blanket of fog lifts.

During this grueling time, I strained a back muscle under my left shoulder blade. *Oh, great! Now that I can see to paddle, I'm suffering from a backache.* The pain intensifies the farther I go. I pull over and lie down for fifteen minutes on the sand to give my back a break. Whether I lay, sit, or stand, I find no comfortable position. *Well, if it hurts while I'm resting, I may as well be paddling.* After taking a couple ibuprofens, I get right back into my kayak and continue paddling.

I face yet another obstacle—the wind. It has intensified significantly, so much so, it is a struggle to paddle downstream.

This afternoon I experience my first emotional low. "I hate this rotten river!" I yell out, frustrated with the morning fog, an aching back, endless bends in the river and wind stronger than the current. I lash out, striking the water with my paddle as hard as I can, spraying water over my deck. "There," I say, taking a deep breath, "that feels better." *Now, Byron Curtis, get over it and continue on. There is no time for childishness. Focus on your goal.*

To take my mind off the wind that continues to jerk at my paddle, I plan what I will eat for supper—*something other than rice—powdered eggs—smooth, creamy eggs (I might even scrounge up a packet of ketchup or two)—and for dessert, peanut butter and honey.* My mouth waters.

My attention is distracted by a small aircraft, swooping down and disappearing behind a line of trees along the riverbank. Seconds later, it makes a near vertical ascent. I watch the crop duster dive and climb time after time, changing directions over the river and eventually directly overhead. *The guy behind the controls would make an excellent fighter pilot.*

The crop duster entertains me for a good hour. *I wonder how much of the chemical he sprays makes its way into the Mississippi?* This is a good reason not to drink it.

It isn't much longer before I have another diversion. I spy something small and red floating in the water. Paddling up to it, I recognize it to be an apple. *Ripe, juicy fruit would taste really good right now.* I pluck it out of the water, feeling its firmness. *It may have fallen off a barge. As much as I'd like to eat it, I'd better pass.* So to remember it, I set it afloat and snap a quick picture. *I'll buy an apple someday from the local orchards when I return home.*

Many barges pass me on the river today. The largest ones usually have forty-two barges joined together. If it isn't for tows and their cargo, I would say there isn't any civilization along this stretch of the Mississippi River. This is a very remote river here in the south, and I prefer it this way.

I stop for the night after paddling forty-six miles. As planned, I prepare eggs for supper, and yes, I am able to spice them up with ketchup. Later, while washing the water line off my kayak, I run my hand along the duct tape. *It's still holding tight.* This reminds me of an experience I had in Alaska.

> *A bush pilot friend flew my brother and me into the wilderness to hunt moose. While loading his Piper Pacer, I accidentally jabbed a two-inch hole through the canvas skin of the plane with the frame of my backpack. In showing the pilot, he said to leave the pack sticking through the canvas and tie it securely in place. After landing and removing the back-pack, the pilot slapped a few pieces of duct tape—or hundred-mile-an-hour tape, as he called it—over the hole. It was still holding when he flew the moose meat and us out four days later.*

Before bed, I doctor up the cuts on my fingers with more antibiotic cream and new dressings. I write in my journal as I'm serenaded by the howls and yips of coyotes calling to one another.

I trail off to sleep with the songs of coyotes being sung in the distance and visions of good times in Alaska.

Day 29

N. 35° 44' 54"
W. 89° 49' 29"

My eyes strain to focus in the dark. It will be light soon. The urge to paddle pulls my thinning body from the warmth of my sleeping bag. A chill in the morning air sends goose bumps running up and down my arms and back. Realizing my body will warm up soon after I begin paddling, I dress in layers.

All is quiet. Unlike the wooded sites of the northern Mississippi River, no birds greet me with their songs on the endless dunes. On the up side, I don't hear the song of the mosquito either. As if to signal the official start of a new day, a coyote gives a lone howl.

According to my calendar and maps, I have paddled approximately 900 miles in four weeks. I have approximately 800 miles left to go. If I can accomplish close to fifty miles each day, realistically, I could arrive in Morgan City, Louisiana, in fifteen or sixteen days. But I won't reach my goal by looking at maps or thinking about it; I must press on. With a renewed sense of accomplishment, I paddle with vigor.

Not only am I more than half way, mileage wise, but also I have passed through six of ten states. With Arkansas on my right and Tennessee to my left, I pass high banks, chock-full of flowing greens. Thick hardwood forests stand strong and tall; the smells of the fall haven't taken hold yet. I soak in the beauty, as I paddle by at an absorbing pace.

I am treated to a straight section in the river. Not only is it easier for me, but the river's current seems to enjoy its freedom also. If this continues, I should reach Memphis, Tennessee, tomorrow.

My mouth waters and my stomach pangs with hunger, reminding me it is time for a lunch snack. A vanilla Power Bar and a drink of presweetened Kool-Aid should do the trick.

Most of the towns are hidden from my view now. The map indicates their existence, but the landscape, from my position, yields no evidence of their being there. I haven't seen anyone to speak to in, it must be, two days now.

I spend most of my day paddling in the main channel, catching the fastest flow of water. Sometimes the channel is in the middle of the river; sometimes it makes its way close to shore. When this happens, I look toward the riverbank and am encouraged when the vegetation passes in a blur. I check my GPS; it reads seven, sometimes eight miles per hour. Today I squeeze out forty-seven miles.

Most of the day, my body is hot and sweaty from being in the confines of my kayak. A mile-long sandbar seems like a good place to stop for the night. I quickly make for the beach and pull my kayak up on shore. I take a 360 degree-look around. Nothing but sand and river surrounds me. This is so unlike me, but I have had enough of these sweaty, itchy and constricting clothes, so I take them off—all of them. Since I can see in every direction, I feel it is safe to go about my daily camp chores in the nude. Immediately, I rinse my clothes out in the river and hang them over my kayak and over my paddle, sticking upright into the sand. Because of the slight breeze and warm sun, they should dry quickly.

Next, I move to the task of setting up my tent. I retrieve my sleeping pad and bag and toss them into the tent. I look for something heavy to rest on top of a stake that keeps working loose. As I return to the tent with a piece of driftwood, I bend down to put it in place.

"Ooooooh weeee!" My head snaps around toward the voices from the river. Two men with scraggly hair look at me from a barge making its way upstream. "Ooooooh weeee!" they call again.

Instantly, I feel vulnerable and unprotected standing there naked. I sprint for my tent and dive inside headfirst. After the barge passes, I peek out from the tent door. All is clear. I scramble to my clothes that are, by now, almost dry and put them on. *I guess I will need to carefully choose the next place and time I wear my birthday suit.*

Day 30

N. 35° 18' 17"
W. 90° 06' 07"

At 5:00 a.m., howling coyotes again wake me. They are very close this morning—only 100 yards away—closer than they ever have been. Sometimes they sound like hyenas, yipping and yelping, even laughing.

Leaving my campsite ten miles north of Memphis, I reach the edge of town in exactly two hours. I share the river with barge traffic only. According to the map and Mike's directions, I will have to paddle around the bottom of Mud Island and head north up a man-made channel to find a marina near the overhead bridge. Making my way around the southern point, I face the city of Memphis, with tall buildings looming ahead—one looks like a pyramid. Mud Island Marina and Yacht Club rests less than a mile up the channel. It is the first marina since Hoppies and smaller than I had pictured it in my mind. Nonetheless, I am glad to see it. I pull up slowly to the floating docks. Like Hoppies, all seems still and quiet. I paddle to the next dock. With his back to me, a man sits with his feet resting on a table. In one hand he holds a cordless phone, into which he is talking. In the other, he holds a cell phone. I nudge the bow of my kayak into the dock, three feet from where the man sits; it seems he is unaware of my presence. "Excuse me, Sir." He doesn't respond. "Excuse me, Sir," I repeat, this time more loudly.

"Yeah?" he responds, turning around quickly.

"Is it okay if I tie up here to get some water and use the phone?"

"Well, sure. It will be easier for you to get out over there," he says, pointing to the shoreline.

I land where he suggested and with water bags in hand, I walk over to the marina office. Another man, quiet and of few words, shows me a spigot where I can fill up with water. I also make a quick call to Wendi from the pay phone. While I am here,

I use the restroom and wash up a bit using soap and warm water. *Boy, does that feel good!* Even though the marina is small, it is nicely stocked with a variety of drinks. I purchase three juices, a six-pack of Mt. Dew and two personal-size bags of chips, all of which I will ration for three days.

"How far down river till the next marina?" I ask, as I pay the attendant eleven dollars.

"Let me see. I think it might be Greenville, Mississippi." The attendant turns to yell to a man behind a glass window twenty feet away. I can't hear the man's reply, so I pick up my snacks and approach the glass. The manager slides the window open. "Are you the fellow that came in that ca-noe?" He spoke with a thick southern drawl.

"That's me."

"Did you come from up the river?" he questions.

"Yes."

"Did you have any troubles up there?"

"No. Everything went okay."

"You're lucky. Whenever there's trouble on the river, it's always from up there."

"What kind of trouble?" I ask.

"Lots of trouble. Everything from robberies to murders," he replies.

"Well, then I'm glad I'm past that part."

"You'll have it better to the south of here. More people and better going."

I'm glad to hear that.

"The next marina you should come to is in Greenville."

"How many miles away would that be?"

"About a hundred, I think. Yeah, about a hundred miles."

I thank him for the information and head back out to my red ca-noe. *I guess I'm fortunate to be alive after coming from "up the river."*

I savor each drink of the Mt. Dew and each bite of ranch flavored Doritos. Carefully, I stash the rest of the snacks in my kayak before paddling out of the small harbor and back down the channel to the river.

By the time I make it back to the main channel, the wind has picked up tremendously. It jerks and pulls on my paddle, trying to rip it from my hands. We struggle back and forth, neither one giving in. I am at war with the wind; every stroke's a battle.

Other than the unyielding wind, the weather has been dry—pleasant for outdoor camping. It has been two and a half weeks since rain dampened my trip. *How long will this trend continue?*

It is 5:00 p.m. and I have been in my kayak for seven hours. I am just shy of a fifty-mile day according to my maps and GPS. On the downstream side of a rock dike, I discover a natural marina. Several sand spits, approximately fifteen feet wide, thirty feet long and three feet high, protrude from the wall, creating lagoons just the right size to anchor small boats. I claim the end sandbar as my resting place for this evening.

A very unique camp on the lower Mississippi River.

Day 31

N. 34° 49' 06"

W. 90° 26' 29"

The serenity of the night was broken by a Great Blue Heron with a bad attitude. Throughout the night and into the early morning hours, the bird flew over my camp, squawking as if I was invading its territory. When I push off at 6:30 a.m., he is still a nuisance. All is not lost, as I am greeted by a full moon over the west bank and a brilliant sunrise in the east.

"He's doing it again!" This is a phrase my son uses to inform Mom that I'm wrestling with him. This time it is I who is saying, "It's doing it again!" but I'm talking about the wind blowing directly into my face.

If the wind's mission is to force me off the water, it is a futile goal. It would be nice to have a radio, to take my mind off the annoying wind, but I have no extra room for luxury items. Maybe if I had a motor, I could laugh at the wind. The more the wind would blow, the more I would open the throttle—that is, until the gas ran out, I damaged the prop or needed new spark plugs. With a motor there is always the cost of maintenance and repairs. I'll stick with my radio-free kayak.

Each day the river grows more remote. Today, the only evidence of life I see is a passing barge. Most of the time I can't see the crew, but I know they must be there. I feel like I will never see humanity again.

I paddle fifty-three miles before finding a Mississippi River paradise. The wide and flat, pristine beach drops off sharply into the river. The shadows of nearby shade trees stripe the shore. I pitch my tent on a high spot and admire the spectacular view of the river. *I think this is one of my favorite locations so far.*

I sit at my perfect campsite soaking up the moment before darkness encases me. Today I reach two milestones—one thousand miles and a new state line, Mississippi, which touches the Gulf. In the beginning, the thought of the end was too disheartening; I had to take one day at a time. Now that I'm getting closer to the Gulf, I am confident that I will realize my goal.

The silence is broken by a whoosh of several hundred pelicans gracefully gliding over the surface of the water.

I knew it would be a matter of time before the weather forecast called for a significant chance of thunderstorms. I have enjoyed the sun's presence; however, I will welcome the cooler weather. In the thirty-one days of this trip, I have had only six rainy days—what a meteorological blessing. Thank you, God.

Day 32

N. 34° 19' 36"
W. 90° 45' 02"

No squawking bird kept me up last night. I wake, refreshed, but a little apprehensive at what today's weather will hold. I unzip the tent fly. Peeking out, I'm greeted by a clear sky filled with brilliant stars. Pleasantly surprised, I quickly stow everything in my kayak.

Within minutes the sky lightens enough for me to paddle. I make my way into the river's current. Paddling around the curve, I'm greeted with a gusty south-southwest wind. I push down on the top of my hat and tighten the drawstrings under my chin. "Slow and steady. Steady and slow." This will be my motto today.

At 10:30 a.m. I notice quite a bit of logging activity taking place along the riverbanks. A crane is loading logs onto two barges parked along the shore. Every now and then a log falls into the river creating a huge splash. At the same time, a northbound tow, pushing forty-two barges and kicking a good-sized wave out the back, will soon be passing the two parked barges. That leaves maybe thirty yards for me to slip between them. This does not allow any room for logs that miss their target and crash into the river. Small beads of sweat quickly develop on my forehead.

Holding my breath, I squeeze between the moving and parked barges. As I am half-way through the ordeal, the crane operator shuts off his engine. I turn to look as he opens his door.

"Where you coming from?" he yells out.

"Wisconsin."

"You ever been to Black River Falls?"

By this time I drift out of hearing distance, so we give each other a wave. Thankfully he waits until I am free from the canyon created by the barges before returning to the task of loading logs.

At noon, I pass parallel to an incredibly, long sandbar. I catch a glimpse of something moving a half-mile ahead. As the distance between us lessens, the coyote sits down to watch me. I am surprised that he shows no fear, considering he is at least three-quarters of a mile from the safety of the trees. I stop paddling and our eyes lock on like lasers. Eventually, he raises and slowly trots back up the sandbar.

At 1:30 p.m., while paddling along the Arkansas riverbank, I see a mile marker and decide to check my mileage. I am 200 yards away when I notice a black object near the marker. I am unsure of what it is until it moves. This is my first black bear siting of my trip. I pull out my camera hoping to get a picture. Thinking I am close enough, I look through the eyepiece of the camera seeing only a small, black dot. The following message should be printed on the corner of pictures taken by point-and-shoot cameras: OBJECTS IN PICTURE ARE CLOSER THAN THEY APPEAR. Deciding against wasting a picture, I simply watch the bear as it meanders into the brush. Spotting this black bear intensifies my feeling of isolation.

The wind continues today, whipping giant clouds of sand into a frenzy. Despite its attempts to slow me down, I keep a persistent pace, eating up forty miles. Remembering last night's weather forecast calling for thunderstorms, I monitor the western sky as dark clouds pile up and approach quickly.

I frantically search for tree cover, hoping the storm doesn't catch me. Rumble! Thunder warns me of approaching danger. I look to the west side—rocks, jagged rocks, as far as I can see. My eyes dart to the eastern shore—long, flat sandbars stretching for miles. Tempest, blue-black clouds are upon me. Crack! Boom! I can feel the lightning bearing down on me. Realizing I am the tallest object for at least a mile in every direction, I paddle like a mad man, digging my paddle in deep and furious. Crash! Lightning splits the sky. I imagine getting struck by lightning each time I lift my paddle. The storm descends upon me violently. The westerly winds shooting dart-like rains into my right side. *I must get off the water! I need something to hide behind!*

My eyes frantically search for shelter, as I paddle with all my might. A four-foot high sandbar welcomes me as I round a small bend in the river. Recognizing that this dune is my only option, I ram the bow of my kayak against the sand. However, the wind, rain and current don't make it easy for me. In one brief second my kayak spins around, facing me upstream. Still against the shore, I leap from my kayak. Grabbing the bowline, I lean back sharply, heaving my weighted kayak twenty feet up onto the sand.

I bundle up in my rain suit, even though I am already soaking wet from the driving rains. Crack! The fierce lightning forces me to lay flat, head down, next to my kayak. Pelted by angry wind and driving rain, and threatened by wicked lightning, I wait in this prone position for forty minutes.

As the weather begins to calm, I lift my head to investigate my situation. The rain is falling lightly now, the lightning has moved on, and the wind has subsided. It is starting to get late and pitch darkness will be upon me in less than an hour. I make my mind up to stay here for the night.

The rain stops long enough for me to pitch my tent in a three-foot gully protecting me from a westerly wind. I waste no time getting inside my tent and removing my wet clothes. I put water on the stove to boil and gobble down a few handfuls of trail mix. After drinking a cup of hot chocolate, I wrap up with my sleeping bag to get warm, while listening to raindrops beat a rhythm on my tent.

While writing in my journal, I detect a change in the wind direction. No longer protected, my small tent is now in direct line of the frigid northerly winds. I have difficulty sleeping. As I doze,

I am awakened by a huge gust. I am concerned about my kayak, as there is nothing to tie it to. A gust of wind could blow it into the river. Dressed only in my underwear, I slip out of the tent and snuggle my kayak next to my tent.

The rain stops and the clouds disperse, but the wind intensifies, pelting sand at my tent. I am forced to sit up on my knees and press my hands against the north side to keep the tent wall from sagging in and breaking the aluminum tent poles. The wind does not give up. My arms grow weary and slide down the tent wall. I slump over and doze. The wind gusts, startling me to alertness like the swerve of a car jolts its sleeping driver back to consciousness. With wide eyes and a stiff posture, I once again get back to work, keeping the tent walls from caving in. But soon my tired arms and body droop and I nod off again. This tormenting scenario continues for hours.

Day 33

N. 33° 57' 21"
W. 91° 04' 47"

By midnight, the north wind has cooled the air temperature to fifty degrees. Shivering, I put on my damp clothes. Another gust bears down on my tent. I hear the kayak moving around. Understanding the seriousness of losing my transportation, I quickly slip outside the tent. In the moonlight, I see that the kayak has moved only a little, but a little is too far for me. After securing the loosening tent stakes, I take the bowline that is still attached to the kayak into the tent with me and tie it to my lifejacket. *If the wind wants my kayak, it will have to pull my lifejacket through the zipped door first.*

With the air temperature continuing to drop, I return to my post and battle against the wind for another two hours. Between gusts, I crawl into my sleeping bag in an attempt to warm my shivering body. My efforts are futile, as my damp clothes are sucking the warmth from my body. I put on my headlamp and exit the tent, braving the sandstorm once again. Drifts of sand are building up against my tent and kayak. Shivering, I work quickly, digging through the bags in my kayak searching for dry clothes. Without hesitation, I scramble back into the tent and replace my damp clothing with warm fleece. It is 3:00 a.m., and for the first time I am able to relax.

Trying to ignore the wind gusts, I doze in and out of sleep for two and a half hours. I wake at 5:30 a.m. desperate to leave this place.

Sand is everywhere—in my tent, my kayak, my clothes and even my ears. As I pack in the dark, I listen to the early morning weather forecast. I know it is cooler than the forty-two-degree air temperature, because the wind is still howling.

At 6:30 a.m., there's just enough daylight to take off. The only advantage to a northerly wind is that it's at my back, pushing me toward my goal. At this point, I estimate four or five days of paddling the Mississippi River before cutting off onto the Atchafalaya River. This means I could make it to the Gulf in potentially nine days.

I paddle relentlessly throughout the day, listening often to NOAA weather radio. Hurricanes and tropical storms are being tracked off the coast of Mexico. If they make their way up the

Gulf, they could greatly affect my weather situation. But right now, I'm taking advantage of the wind, which is in my favor.

I am thankful for another fifty-mile day and a protected campsite behind a rock dike—no late night battle with the wind tonight.

It is Saturday, but all I encountered at a distance was two deer and a few barges. I'm really missing home now. Maybe it's because I haven't spoken to anyone in approximately seventy-eight hours. Or maybe it's because I am closer to my goal of reaching the Gulf, and I'm excited that Wendi and Isaac will be in Morgan City, Louisiana, to pick me up.

Day 34

N. 33° 30' 41"
W. 91° 10' 39"

Today I need to replenish my dwindling water supply. I remember that the yacht club manager in Memphis said there was a marina in Greenville, Mississippi, so that's where I'm headed.

With the wind still in my favor, I reach Greenville, twelve miles away, in less than two hours. To get to the marina, however, I will need to paddle four miles up a channel and against the wind.

A couple hundred empty barges line the channel. I see two men on a tow heading up the channel, so I flag them down.

"Where'd you come from?" one asks.

"Wisconsin."

"No way! In that thing?" he replies.

"Could you guys tell me if there's a marina up this channel?"

"Yeah, there's one...a mile or so...on the right-hand side."

It's comforting to know that I'm not chasing after a fictitious marina. I paddle for forty-five minutes and see no sign of the marina. Looking for someone to question, I see a man on the back of a moored tow.

As he is repainting the boat's name, I ask, "Do you know if there's a marina ahead?"

"I'm not really sure," he replies. "I'm not from around here. I just work on this tow."

"Do you have any drinking water that I could have?"

"Where do you put water in that thing anyway?"

"I have some water bags. I only need about two and a half gallons."

"The water we got isn't much better than this water." He points to the river. "We have to buy our water and you'll have to ask those guys for it." He points further up the tow to a couple of guys wearing hard hats. In frustration, I keep paddling northward.

Soon, I approach a docked Coast Guard boat named PATOKA. Hoping the crew will be more helpful than the last guy, I yell, "Patoka!" Two Coast Guard servicemen scrambled onto the deck.

"Yes?" puffs one man.

"I have some questions for you." My voice is deep and serious. The men approach the railing. "I'm paddling from Wisconsin to the Gulf."

They look at each other in disbelief. "You mean you came all this way in that little thing?" the one wearing sunglasses questions.

"That's a long way," the other comments.

"Can you fellows tell me if there's a marina up this channel and how far it is?"

"It's only a couple hundred yards up," says one. The other nods. They both point north.

"Have you ever been on the Atchafalaya River in Louisiana?" I ask.

"We were on it two years ago, feeding cabbage to the alligators," one says, turning to the other for confirmation.

"Great," I sigh, "let's hope they don't think I'm a piece of cabbage." They laugh.

"Some of those gators are about as big as your kayak," jokes the man with sunglasses resting on the top of his head. We all laughed.

I take their picture and thank them both for their service in the military. I press on in search of the illusive marina, which is more than a couple hundred yards up. Still, I trust the advise of others and keep going. Finally, one mile later, a casino boat is anchored beyond the marina.

I paddle into the marina where all seems dead. There is no one at the fueling station or anywhere else, for that matter. I take the liberty of finding a water spigot and filling up my water bags.

As my containers are about full, a man approaches. "If you need anything," he says, "you can go into that building over there. One of the back doors should be open."

Needing a phone, I take his advice. The first door is locked, but the second is not. I open the door and enter a banquet hall of sorts.

"Hello? Is anyone here?"

An elderly lady emerges from a back room.

"Excuse me," I begin. "Do you have a pay phone I can use?"

"No. We just have a regular phone. Do you need long distance?"

"Yes, but I have a calling card."

"Well, that's okay, I guess, if you use a calling card."

"I'm traveling down the river and would like to call home."

"Several canoers have stopped here. It's getting awful late in the year, though, isn't it? It's cold at night. I hope you have a jacket?"

She leads me through the banquet hall to a bar. From the phone, I make a call home. Wendi has been following my progress on the map, as well as keeping the local newspaper informed of my happenings. She is also concerned about the severe weather to my south. As quickly as I can, I recall the storm from the night before. Eager to get going, so that I can talk to her face to face, I cut the conversation short, promising to call as soon as I get the chance.

After hanging up the phone I ask the lady, "Do you have any food I can buy?"

"I'm sorry, honey," she says. "All we have are chips." She holds up a snack-size bag.

"I'll take four bags." All of them are outdated, but I don't care. "How about pop?" I question.

"Well, we only have Sprite or Diet Coke."

"I'll take six Sprites, please." I don't need anything diet right now.

The kind lady bags my purchases. "Be careful and don't freeze," she warns.

"Thank you. I'll be careful."

As I'm returning to my kayak, I stop at the spigot and drink all the water my stomach can hold. Back down the current-less channel I paddle, passing the hundreds of parked barges. Approaching the end of the canal, excitement returns, as I know I will be making progress once again down the Mississippi. However, a channel dredge blocking the quarter-mile wide canal soon squelches the feeling. *Now what do I do?*

I look left, and then right, for someone, anyone. I spy a man on the dredging equipment and paddle toward him. I shrug my shoulders and point one way and then the other. He waves to acknowledge me and disappears through a small door of the pilothouse. Five seconds later he appears and motions me to the left. I proceed cautiously. Only five feet to my right a huge dredging bit surfaces from the channel's muddy water. It looks like a dinosaur head coming up for air. Without hesitation, I pass quickly. Giving a thankful and relieved wave, I safely reach the river.

The river's personality changes once again. It's as if two giants pick up the land on either side of the river and pull against each other, widening the river and smoothing the hills flat.

I don't have a sandbar to camp on tonight. I pitch my tent in the edge of a willow forest next to a muddy bank. I don't care; I'm getting close to the end.

Day 35

N. 33° 07' 30"
W. 91° 06' 24"

I begin early, as I have to make up for lost time spent getting water in Greenville yesterday. I have paddled farther than the length of the Iditarod dogsled race, which is about 1,100 miles. I don't face the cold like they do, but I don't have a team of dogs to help me with the miles either. Thinking of completing Arkansas and passing into Louisiana, my final state, or paddling farther than the length of the Iditarod, encourages me to keep going, knowing I will finish soon.

Before pushing off, I collect trail mix, Kool-Aid and a baggy of instant potatoes and store them in my cockpit. (Like oatmeal, I add cold water to instant potatoes, squish them around in my hand and suck them out of the bag.) I plan to have lunch on the go today, challenging my body to stay in the kayak as long as the weather is favorable. After today, it looks as though I will be plagued with thunderstorms for a week—maybe for the rest of my journey.

This evening I camp on the Louisiana side. It is getting difficult to find adequate sites now that the land is lower and wetter. It seems, at about 3:00 p.m., when I'm not ready to quit for the night, I find a decent place for a tent. But when I need to stop, at about 4:30 p.m., the picking gets slim.

Unable to see mile markers today, I'm not sure how far I paddled. What I do know is that I spent ten hours and fifteen minutes in the kayak without getting out once. That is a long, long time to be confined to a sitting position. I did have to do a good bit of shifting around to find a comfortable spot, as my backside gets bonier each day.

As I write in my journal tonight I think of my family—my wife and son, mom and dad, brother and sisters, along with their families and my in-laws. I miss them all and think of them often.

Day 36

N. 32° 34' 31"
W. 91° 07' 22"

This morning, my tired body wakes to the sound of the wind snapping the taut edges of my tent. The drive to finish is great, so in spite of the wind, I pack up and begin my thirty-sixth day.

For hours, I struggle faithfully against the southeastern blast, as it creates two-foot waves quartering at me on the right. Late morning, I reach Vicksburg, Mississippi. Looking up at the town, I reflect briefly on its awesome history. It's incredible to think that here, on these very riverbanks, a crucial battle of the Civil War was fought in 1863.

> *The forces of the Union Army attacked this southern city, knowing a victory here would give them control over the entire Mississippi River. It would also split the Confederate forces in half, fragmenting their strength. The Confederate Army knew that a loss would be devastating.*

The siege of Vicksburg took several months to complete. I imagine the smell of gunpowder, the sound of rifle fire, and soldiers from both Armies marching up and down the riverbanks. I imagine many men lying dead along these banks as the Union forces won the battle of Vicksburg.

It is now 138 years later as I paddle past this historic town. The river and its banks are alive with activity, much different and more peaceful than in 1863.

This morning the sky was overcast. The same constant gray color covered the entire sky. Now the clouds are thickening, forming shapes and dark shadows. So after passing Vicksburg, I check the radio for a weather update. The projected forecast for about a week is showers and thunderstorms. The bad news is the rest of my trip may be soggy, but the good news is I can refill my water containers with filtered rainwater, if I need to.

For lunch I devour another bag of instant potatoes and my last can of pop from Greenville. The food bags are getting lighter and more compact. My remaining staples include instant potatoes, rice and bullion cubes, cream of wheat, four Power Bars, some powdered eggs, dried apricots and trail mix.

Most of the fat is gone from my butt. It is extremely painful when my bones rub hard on the fiberglass kayak seat. The kayak, including its comfortable seat, has performed well; it has done all I have asked of it.

Water is beginning to seep through the crack in the hull from the rapids near the Middle Bar island, but it continues to float all my gear and me down this long river. Each evening I soak up the half-cup of water with a sponge and wring it out on the ground. I'll patch the crack properly when I get home.

Today I swallowed up only thirty-five miles, even though I paddled nine and a half hours without getting out of the kayak. A three-and-a-half-mile average tells me the wind was much more effective than the current today. This evening I am blessed to find a dike campsite, where I get a reprieve from the wind.

Day 37

N. 32° 09' 38"
W. 90° 59' 46"

I did some mileage calculations last night. Since the start of this voyage until now, I have averaged thirty-nine miles a day. I have not been able to maintain the fifty-mile average I had hoped for after passing St. Louis. I believe this is due to the fact that the river is wider and that the wind has been brutal for five consecutive days. I can at least expect to conquer thirty-five to forty-five miles each day—not too bad considering the odds.

I plan another meal-on-the-go today, as thunderstorms brew to the north of me. I seem to be staying just ahead of them. Eventually, they will catch me, but maybe I can prolong the inevitable a bit longer.

I continue on at a strong, steady pace. I sing out, occasionally, trying to drown out the wind. Sometimes I paddle in silence, thinking about home or food. Other times I concentrate on each paddle stroke, as though watching arms on a machine move in precisely the same hypnotic motion.

My stomach growls, reminding me it's lunch time. *What shall I have? Hot deep-dish pizza? Fried chicken or fish with all the fixings?* Right now, cold instant potatoes and a few dried apricots will have to suffice. I gobble them down as if it is the only meal I've had in days. I hurry for no other reason than to beat the thunderstorm.

I paddle hard and continuous until 2:30 p.m. Without warning, gruesome, gray-green clouds appear from beyond the trees, like a wild cat waiting in the tall grass for just the precise moment to attack. Feverishly, I scan the shore for refuge, finding only rocks on one side and slimy mud on the other side. *There's got to be something around this bend.* Sure enough, a quarter-mile ahead, a small sandy beach appears.

I paddle with all my might to reach the landing before the storm engulfs me. Just as I reach the beach, swirling winds hit me full force, like a surprise attach in a back alley. I leap from the kayak, tying it to a nearby rock. Grabbing as much as I can carry—tent, sleeping bag and other necessary gear—I run up the riverbank for cover.

The eerie green sky looms all around as the gale continues. *Looks like tornado clouds to me.* I run through long grass and eight-foot willow trees, finding an opening under dense cover that's large enough for my tent. Erecting it in record time, I throw the rain fly into place just as rain begins to pour. I secure the fly as best I can before falling into the tent.

Driving rain pounds my tiny shelter. Remembering the storm that kept me awake through most of the night, I sit alert, ready to brace myself against the tent walls. The willows and grass snap like whips at my tent. Only two thin layers of nylon separate me from the danger outside. I remember my kayak, exposed and unprotected.

Because the wind is from the southwest, the air temperature is considerably warmer than the last storm I encountered. Outside it is eighty degrees. Inside my tent it is hot and humid; my clothes are damp with sweat. *I'm not looking forward to being cramped in here all afternoon and night.* I strip down to my underwear to wait out the long, muggy night.

Thunder sounds off in the distance occasionally, but it is still raining. I look at my watch; it is 4:39 p.m. *This waiting-out-the-storm business sure makes a guy hungry.* I put water on the stove to boil. After eating two servings of Cream of Wheat, I fall asleep for about an hour.

I wake before the last few minutes of obscured daylight fade. Listening to the quiet rain, I lay looking up at the tent ceiling. *What's that black thing?* I reach my hand up and the black thing moves. I turn on my headlamp to have a better look. *A spider! A huge, black spider with black, penetrating eyes!* As the beam of light shines on it, the spider draws into a tight ball. As I've said before, I don't care for spiders and I certainly don't want to share my tent with one that big. Finding a damp wad of tissue paper in my pocket, I plan my attack. I'll just simply squish the beady-eyed beast. Stealthily, I reach up and grab it. "That was easy," I boast. I squeeze the tissue in my hand. Slowly and carefully I open the tissue to see if the spider is dead. Not only is it not dead, it isn't there! *The beast gave me the slip. Oh, great! How am I supposed to sleep tonight knowing that an enormous, eight-legged creature is on the loose? If I don't hunt it down, I will be tormented all night by arachniphobia.*

With determined eyes I search for ten minutes, looking here and there, under this and that. *I know it's watching me from a protected vantage point... Where are you?* Suddenly, I spot it crouching on my sleeping bag, inches from where I lay my head. My eyes peer at it. *This time you won't escape.* With tissue in hand, I pounce with all the speed I can muster. This time I know I get him. I squish the tissue, feeling and hearing its body crunch between my fingers. *Now I can rest easy.*

Day 38

N. 31° 48' 57"
W. 91° 20' 57"

Sometime during the night the rain stopped; the wind eased up, also. Well rested, I break camp and load all my gear back into my boat. Before removing the cockpit cover, I filter the captured rainwater through the hand filter and into a water container. Determined to cover many miles today, I depart, diligently look for areas with swift current.

Three tom turkeys grace a green grassy shoreline. I glide by without a sound, so as not to disturb their strutting and showing off.

Later, I stop paddling long enough to take a long drink of water and check the map and GPS; I need water and it looks as though Natchez, Mississippi, is my next option. I hope it has a friendly landing area and that I won't have to paddle upstream to get to it.

It is mid-morning when I come to Natchez. Using binoculars, I scan its banks, spying a long cement ramp for boats.

The boat ramp at Natchez, Mississippi, during very low water conditions.

The low water level exposes jagged rocks rendering the ramp useless for powerboat and trailer launching, but for me, it will suffice. I land and secure my kayak to one of the larger rocks. Nearby, a ten-foot, old, aluminum canoe is chained down; it looks as though it has been imprisoned for years. Carrying my water bags, I wander up the long, cement grade. Seven or eight historic-looking buildings line the top of this first hill. If I am able to find water here, it will save me a trip to the newer section of town, which appears to be on top of the next hill.

I pass the first red brick building where gifts are sold. As I enter the doorway of the second, a saloon, I am transported into the past. The old, wooden floor creaks as I walk across it to the bar. A man stands behind the bar, his image reflected in a large, antique mirror.

"Good morning," I say, my voice creaking like the wooden floor. It has been four days since I've spoken to anyone.

"Good morning," he responds. "Can I get you anything?"

"I'd like a Coke, please."

He fills a Styrofoam cup with ice and Coke. I chug it down quickly. "You're the first person I've spoken to in days."

"You come off the river?"

"I sure did."

"Big boat?" I bet they don't get many small boats anchoring here.

"No, just a kayak."

"From where?" He empties my water bags and refills them with fresh water from the tap.

"Prescott, Wisconsin. That's up by Minneapolis, Minnesota."

"Takes a brave man to do a trip like that," he says. "I'd sure like to do it sometime."

I throw two small bags of nuts onto the bar to add to my tab.

"I've been in Natchez a long time.... Yep, Natchez, Natchez, Natchez." He pours me another Coke.

We speak for another minute before he is called to the back. Unable to sit on a stool, because my seat hurts too badly, I wander the saloon, looking at the antiques that surround me. The tables, the chairs, the pictures, the bar, even the mirror behind the bar look a hundred years old.

While the bartender is gone, I find a pay phone in a side room and call Wendi. With enthusiasm, she encourages me. "You're almost done! You can do it!"

Am I really almost finished? Her words resound in my ears and inspire my heart.

Assuring her that I'll call when I get to the Atchafalaya River, we say, "good-bye," once again.

I return to the bar. The bartender is back from his errand.

"How old is this place?" I ask.

"A hundred and sixty years."

I order a third Coke and pay the man. I include a three-dollar tip for kindly filling my water bags for me.

"Have you seen the weather forecast?" he asks.

I haven't seen a weather broadcast since Cape Girardeau, Missouri.

"Come over here." He leads me into another room with a television. He turns it to the weather channel and hands me the remote. "Watch this for as long as you like."

He leaves me to watch the satellite image of a large, stormy weather system approaching from the west. Right now it's over Texas, but it will get here all too soon. This news takes the joy right out of my upbeat conversation I just had with Wendi.

As I leave, the man warns, "You be careful. That river's big and rough down past here."

As I carry the water bags to my kayak, I munch down a bag of peanuts. I calculate that I've spent only fifty-three dollars on this trip so far. *That's pretty good, considering I've been away from home for thirty-eight days.*

I don't waste any time getting back to my kayak. I look around; the sky is cloudy, but no rain yet. Most of the dark clouds are to the north. With the goal of reaching the cutoff before it rains, I depart quickly.

Another afternoon comes and goes. Plenty of clouds fill the sky, but no rain yet. Unable to find a sandbar, I camp in the trees on a muddy bank.

Because I am able to leisurely set up camp tonight, I enjoy the last ninety minutes of light by scouting the woods. There are a lot of insects out and about, but none are biting me. I crouch down to spy on a spider making a web—an incredible display of workmanship, with each section perfectly shaped. It didn't take the spider long to complete its creation. I walk through the grass looking for small bugs, thinking I will help the spider find supper. I catch a tiny insect and gently toss it into the web. The spider instantly responds by wrapping the insect in a silky, mummy-like coffin. *Going to save this one for later?* As I continue walking, I notice a dozen or more webs. I am entertained for the rest of the evening catching small insects and throwing them into the webs.

Before retiring, I read from my book and listen to the VHF marine forecast. I drift off to sleep, reflecting upon the day.

Day 39

N. 31° 20' 44"
W. 91° 29' 40"

Mosquitoes descend upon me in full force as I exit the tent. I run to the kayak for insect repellent, which holds them at bay while I break down camp.

Still expecting to paddle in the rain, I am pleasantly surprised that the spongy clouds haven't released their water yet. But when they do, I expect nothing less than a deluge.

I take a short break from my kayak this afternoon. I wander along a low, grassy bank with a backdrop of dense willows. My rest stop is quickly disturbed by an attack of swarming mosquitoes. Soon I am back in my kayak, shifting in the seat, trying to find a comfortable position. If I stretch out my legs and lean back to lift my butt off the seat for a few seconds, this relieves the annoying pain for a while. But it isn't too long before the pain returns.

Not much farther down the river, a sleek, chocolate-brown river otter lopes along the shore. In a flash, it slides into the river and zigzags in front of my kayak. Once again, the otter emerges from the river and darts back and forth on the sand. Without a care in the world, it seems, the otter disappears into the river.

A quick check of the map indicates I am close to the outflow channel. It's a dam of sorts that redirects water from the

Mississippi River into the Atchafalaya River. The outflow channel is too dangerous for boats to use, so in order to switch to the Atchafalaya River, I must pass through the old river lock a few miles to the south of the outflow channel.

I should be able to see the outflow channel around the next bend. As the river straightens, a tow with forty-two barges sits perpendicular to the river's flow with its nose against the muddy bank and its back end sticking out into the main channel. Because of its massive size, it blocks a third of the river. Hesitant to go around, I call the tow captain on the radio.

"This is Kayaker calling the tow that is parked on South Palmet Point on the Mississippi State river bank."

"I can't see anyone out there. Where are you?" comes a reply.

"I'm a kayaker about 300 yards up from your bow." I wave my paddle high in the air to get his visual attention.

"I see you now."

"I'm wondering if it's okay to go around you, or what do you want me to do?"

"Well, I'm just about to flip the switch. You stay toward the shore and I'll move back into the channel."

Within a few seconds the big diesel engines roar to life. The captain swings the massive barges out with agility and ease. When we are side by side, the wheelhouse door opens and the captain emerges. He nods and gives me a wave.

From the Mississippi shore, I look to my right at the outflow channel. With binoculars I read a sign that says, "DANGEROUS DRAW. ALL CRAFT STAY TO THE EAST BANK." As the sign commands, I paddle along the east bank.

Final campsite on the Mississippi River before heading onto Louisiana's Atchafalaya River.

However, I will need to get back to the west bank to be in position to pass through the old river lock onto the Atchafalaya River.

My plan is to make one last camp on the Mississippi River tonight, then head over to the Atchafalaya River in the morning. From here, I will have about ten miles to find a campsite. Between the eighth and ninth mile, a small sandbar, surrounded by rocks, appears on the Louisiana bank.

Several emotions wash over me at this moment. I am glad that I made it this far. At times I felt as though I was caught in time, paddling for eternity, but never making progress. Now the goal seems attainable. I feel anxiety as I prepare to leave the river that has afforded me protection—protection from the elements, dangers, and people. I feel safe camping near the river's edge, able to slip into the water in an instant and paddle away from danger. I'm apprehensive about the alligator activity in this enormous swamp. *How prevalent and active are they this time of year?* The amount of private land concerns me as well. I have proven that I can stay in my kayak for an entire day, but can I sleep in it if I'm unable to find a place to camp? Even though I know very little about the Atchafalaya, I'm excited that I will be experiencing new territory—bayou country. It's hard to believe this is my last night here on the Mississippi.

I will be paddling a new river tomorrow; I may as well look my best. I dig out some clean clothes and put them aside for tomorrow morning. I run my callused hands across my bristly whiskered face. Today is my scheduled appointment with the razor. Time to pull out my Precious Moments mirror; I just have to chuckle.

Now that I'm presentable, I focus my thoughts to the new river and the challenges it will bring. *How wide is the Atchafalaya River in comparison to the Mississippi River? How fast is its current? Will there be much boat traffic?* I can always read or ask questions of others, but I find it's never quite the same as experiencing it for myself.

In my journal I write:

Wendi, only a few more long, yet short, days separate our reunion. I am so much looking forward to it. I pray your trip down to Morgan City will be a safe one. Just think, what has taken me forty-some days to accomplish, will take you only two.

Isaac, I bet I can still beat you at arm wrestling. My arms, as you can imagine, have gotten stronger.

It will be a joy to see you both.

Love, Byron and Dad

Day 40

N. 31° 00' 01"
W. 91° 33' 58"

My mind snaps awake to a morning of unknowns. My first call to order is a radio check of today's weather. All is not good. Severe weather, including damaging winds and hail the size of golf balls, is predicted. I leave my tent to take a look around. Ominous thunderclouds surround me on all sides. My small, secure paddling world seems congested with dangers. The big question haunts me. *Should I stay and anchor down in my camp, or should I go and face whatever the weather brings me?* I think of my friend Mickey, a levelheaded man with top-notch judgment. *What would he do in this situation?*

"What would you do, Mick?" I shout, as I stand on the sandy shore looking up at the dismal sky. My wife tells me that one of my strengths is my ability to make quick, yet wise decisions. I pace the sandbar, angry with myself for not being able to make a decision.

I ponder my options a little longer. I come to the conclusion that either the storm will beat me up in camp or on the river. I guess I'll have to choose between the two. Knowing that it's hard for me to stay put and do nothing, I side with the river. With my mind made up, I focus on packing everything up quickly.

I get no further than two hundred yards when the rain starts. Turning the corner, I head toward the lock. The dark, nutrient-rich mud is thickly vegetated. Many gouges scar the banks of the narrow channel where barges rammed up against them. *This would not be a good time to meet a barge.* As I approach the lock, the rain pours down from the sky—tropical storm style.

"Old River Lock and Dam, this is Gulfstream Kayak," I say into my VHF radio.

"This is Old River Lock, where are you?" It is difficult to hear his response over the deafening downpour. I turn the volume button to high.

"I'm a kayaker on the Mississippi River side of the lock." I wave my paddle, hoping the sheets of rain don't veil my signal.

"I see you now."

"I am wondering if there is any way for me to talk to someone about the Atchafalaya River?" The radio is silent.

A different voice says, "What's wrong? Did you forget your rain suit?"

My response is firm. "Sir, I am 1,500 miles from home and I want to know what I'm getting myself into." Again the radio is quiet.

After what seems like minutes, a different voice responds. "You may climb the stairs to the fence at the top. At that point I will instruct you further."

I lift my kayak onto a cement ramp. At the end of the ramp, I climb the half-dozen or more steps to the fence at the top.

"Open the gate and come straight ahead to the door," comes the instructions over the radio.

As instructed, I enter the gate and walk toward the metal door, which opens before I reach it. A man, seated ten feet back from the opening, motions for me to come in. I enter the cold, steely room—a four-by-twelve-foot control room—water dripping off me and onto the white sheet that lay on the floor.

"You're not a terrorist are you?" asks the worker.

"No, sir, I'm not." *Would a terrorist say yes?* "I'm a family man, paddling down this river to the Gulf."

"What do you want to know about the Atchafalaya?" The man leans forward, elbows resting on his knees.

"Well," I start, "what is it like? How much current is there? Are there any dangerous areas? Is there a lot of barge traffic? Do I need to worry about the alligators?"

The man answers my questions with the best knowledge he has of the river. There are a few wing dams on the northern part of the river. The current is relatively the same as the Mississippi's. There is some, but not much, barge traffic. And I need not worry about the alligators; for the most part, they stay in the swamps beyond the channel.

"Do you have any other questions?"

"I was wondering if I could wait out the storm here—somewhere on the grounds?"

"Since 9-11, we're under strict orders from the Federal Government not to have any visitors, I'm sorry, but you can't stay."

"Sir, I was wondering if I could ask one more favor? Is there some way, because of the bad storms, that I could make one phone call home to let my wife know I'm alright?"

He thinks for a moment. Shaking his head, he answers, "I can't let you use this phone because all conversations are taped."

"Do you know of any other way I could call home?" I plead.

He pauses again. "I could take you up to another building… You could make a call from there." He drives me about a quarter-mile to another building. We enter and he shows me the phone. I place a call home to Wendi, who is relieved to hear from me. She has been watching the storms on television and is concerned for my safety. I tell Wendi to leave for Louisiana tomorrow, Sunday, October 14, as I'm 150 miles from the coast and I plan to be in Morgan City in three days. At this point I'm not sure I can paddle three 50-mile days on an unknown river, but I'll do it, if I have to paddle all night.

The lock worker is waiting for me as I hang up the phone. "Do you need anything else?" he asks. "Some drinking water?"

"Sure, I can use some water." He goes into another room and returns with six bottles of water in a plastic, grocery bag.

On the short ride back to the lock, I ask him if he knows of a place I can camp and wait out the weather.

"Well, normally visitors camp on that grassy section over there." He points to the area with lush green grass that I eyed-up earlier. "But since the attacks, we cannot allow it. There is a small place we cleared out, though, about a half-mile away. It's not much, but there are a couple of Port-A-Potties there."

"Port-A-Potties?" To me this means shelter.

He tells me to paddle a short distance east—back the way I came—cross the canal and take a small exit channel, north to a lagoon area.

Before I leave, Ronnie checks the weather for me with the newest satellite images. "I'm afraid I've got bad news," he says. "The weather we have now is only half as bad as what's coming. And it's supposed to get here in about thirty minutes. I wish I could let you stay here, but I can't." I can hear concern in Ronnie's voice. "I wish I could help you out some more."

"I'll see you in the morning to lock me through," I reply.

"I'll be here."

With one hand holding down my hat and the other lugging the bag of water bottles, I sprint to the river. Quickly, I throw the water into the kayak, untie the rope and jump into the cockpit. Pushing off from shore, I take a half-dozen strokes before getting blasted by driving, torrential rains. The wind whips the rain into sheets and slams my kayak into a muddy bank. I imagine my kayak being lifted out of the water by an angry funnel cloud, pitch-poled through the air and slammed into a Louisiana bayou filled with hungry alligators. I lean forward with my head bowed, protecting my face and chest from the storm's fury. In a few moments, I raise my head slightly, each paddle stroke a struggle. I guide my kayak across the river and out a north channel into a lagoon, according to the directions Ronnie gave me.

Up ahead and to the left, the cement boat launch came into view. The fifty-yard ramp rises steeply. Water rushes down it, as if the floodgates are opened. I secure my kayak to a sturdy rock. Afraid the wind will blow my paddle away, I carry it up the bank with me.

A sign at the top reads, "NO CAMPING ALLOWED IN THIS AREA." *What? I thought Ronnie said this was a camping area?* Refusing to give up, I walk a half-mile up the road until I see another sign. It says, "CAMPING THIS WAY."

That's more like it. I traipse in the wind and rain for another quarter-mile. Side by side, like castles in the forest, stand two blue Port-A-Potties—numbers 64 and 220. I open the door to 64. *No way! This is putrid!* I put my hope in 220. Slowly, I open the door. *Yuck! Not much better than 64, but it'll have to do.*

Inside, the air reeks of that fowl Port-A-Potty smell. *But, I'm out of the elements; at least the wind and rain are not hammering me.* Free for the moment, I sit down to rest. I doze off to sleep, but am awakened by the stench and the loud, persistent pounding of the wind-driven rain on the outbuilding. An hour passes, then two. The intensity of the storm diminishes, but the rain continues. I'm not thrilled about my kayak being almost a mile away, so I leave the protection of my shelter to bring it closer.

My temporary shelter, #220, during one of the torrential rain storms in the bayous.

I paddle around a point to get within a hundred yards of the Port-A-Potties. I grab a snack before heading back to my faithful shelter affectionately named *Ol' Blue 220*. After spending another two and a half hours inside the cramped, smelly, plastic container, I have had enough! I poke my head out the door. To the west, four pickup trucks, a camper and a couple of tents huddle around a covered shelter. *I suspect that's where all the campers are. Well, it's time for me to be a visitor.*

I walk toward the camp. When I get to within twenty yards, a man peeks his head out.

"Good morning!" I greet. "Are you taking any visitors?"

"Sure," is his response. "Come on over."

I duck under the canopy that shelters six men—half are dressed in camouflage.

One breaks the silence. "Where'd you come from?"

It's hard not to reply with the same southern drawl. "I came down from Wisconsin in my kayak."

"No way!" one exclaims. "In a little kayak?"

Another speaks, "You must be that fellow that had the paddle leaning up against the outhouse. We thought you was a serial killer waiting for a victim. None of us wanted to come over."

"I was trying to get out of the rain for a while."

"A few years ago," one of the older men adds, "two yachts came through here going all the way to Panama. Now, that's a long trip, but they had big boats. You have only a kayak. You're exposed to all the elements."

Another chimes in, "I gotta hand it to you. You've come a long way. You must be pretty hard. It would be hard enough in a big boat."

Another questions, "Just why *are* you doing this?"

"Well, I love to paddle, for one thing. And for another, I'm doing it for all those who always wanted to, but never had the chance. I'm also doing this trip for my dad who loved the river. And for my son, to show him that he can do things he sets his mind to and to do the things he says he's going to do."

Another one says, "Well, I really respect you for doing it. Lots of people might start a trip like this and when things get tough, they quit. Now you're almost finished. You'll make it."

I appreciate the kind words of encouragement and vote of confidence. Indeed, I am closing in on the goal I have set. If I hang in there a couple more days, the victory of passage will be mine. The comments of these men give me new confidence after being belittled by the terrific storm and by seeking shelter in an outhouse. The words of Gordy ring in my head once again. "Whatever you do, don't quit!"

Another man, shorter and younger than the rest, joins the group. He talks and talks and doesn't pause until he looks at me. "And who are you?" he questions.

"I was about to tell you, but I thought I'd wait 'til you took a breath." Everyone laughs.

The Cajun guys welcome me with shelter, conversation and lunch. I chow down on a chicken salad sandwich and fried sausage. Even though my supply of rice and instant potatoes will last the entire trip, I'm glad for the variety.

I discover that a couple of the guys went to the University of Wisconsin in Madison. When I ask them what they think of the Mississippi River, one says, "Isn't the river up there the size of a ditch?"

"Well, it's a little bigger than that, but not as big as it is down here."

Greg, Frank, Scott, Donald, Evans, Gerald and Toby, the talkative one, have been coming to this spot for four years. They come to hunt squirrel, fish catfish and relax in the woods. They talk of life in Louisiana, a reminder that I'm a visitor in their world.

After spending two and a half hours with these guys, a truck drives up. Ronnie, the lock worker, gets out of the truck.

"A coworker of mine finishes his shift at 2:15 p.m. and is willing to take you to Simmesport, about ten to twelve miles southwest of here," suggests Ronnie.

I like this idea. It means I will bypass the lock and the six-mile canal connecting the two rivers. It'll also save me lost time. I accept Ronnie's offer.

As I wait for Ronnie's coworker, my conversation with the Cajuns continues. Each time the rain lets up, we step out from underneath the tarp to pour kerosene on the smoldering fire. We hover around until it either goes out or the rain puts it out. We perform this little ritual three or four times until we hear a truck coming down the small road.

I walk over to the black, short-bed Chevy truck. Rolling down his window, the driver asks, "Byron, is that you?" His strong southern accent makes my name sound very different—like "Barn."

Robin and I introduce ourselves; I thank him for his kind gesture.

"Oh, that's no problem, Byron."

While Robin turns the truck around, Don walks with me to my kayak. "Do you have a can opener?" he asks in a low voice.

"I have something to open a can."

Don reaches in his coat pocket and secretly produces a can of tuna. "Could you use this?" he whispers.

My mouth waters. "I sure could." He quietly hands it to me and I stuff it in my coat pocket. I'm blessed by this simple, yet thoughtful gift. *I will always remember your kindness. Thanks, Don.*

Now, I'm a bit concerned about how to keep my seventeen-foot kayak in a six-foot truck bed. With the help of the hunting party, we secure my boat to the truck. I leave the kayak loaded with my gear, hoping the extra weight will help hold it in place. I shake hands with each man at the camp, thanking them for their southern hospitality.

As we pass several acres of cotton fields on our way to Simmesport, Robin tells me his philosophy on making a living in this area.

"We do okay. We make a living."

The pouring rain returns. As we approach our destination, Robin offers to take me to a deli for something hot to eat. I accept, eager to prolong my stay in the dry environment.

I attempt to pay Robin for gas, but he refuses. I even offer to buy him something to eat.

"I don't need anything, Byron. You keep your money."

At the deli I order chicken strips, potato wedges and a dinner roll to go. I throw in a couple of Milky Way candy bars—

one for Robin and one for me. It is the least I can give him for his trouble.

"Take it Byron. You need it more than me." This time *I* have none of it. Maybe he'll give it to his daughter, who he talked about.

Back on the road, Robin tells me that he drove a couple, who were canoeing down the river, all the way to Baton Rouge to catch a bus home. They quit and wanted off the river. Robin says I can catch a ride on a barge heading down to Morgan City, but I won't do that; I came to paddle the river. Besides, I'll be finished in a couple of days; it is foolish for me to give up now.

Robin delivers my kayak and me to the boat launch at 4:30 p.m. While backing his truck down the long cement grade to the river, I jot down his name in my logbook, just as I did with all those I met on my expedition. He hands me a lighter, a couple of oranges and two white rags.

"You never know when this stuff will come in handy," he says. "I wish I had more to give you." *You gave me much more than a few tangible things. Thanks, Robin.*

"It's going pretty fast. You be careful, Byron." Robin points to the river's current as he bids me farewell. I return to the river, my sense of adventure renewed by the friends I made today.

It's late, but I'm able to paddle twelve miles and find a small sandbar campsite before is gets dark. I didn't see any signs of private land, but tomorrow's a new day. So far, the Atchafalaya resembles a miniature Mississippi River. In bayou country, I fall asleep a very thankful man.

Day 41

N. 30° 51' 03"
W. 91° 48' 54"

I wake early; all is still and quiet, more so than on the Mississippi. Last night, I made sure my headlamp had fresh batteries, in preparation for nighttime paddling, whether it is early morning or late night. Before the sun has time to think about showing itself, I depart, my headlamp piercing the darkness.

The morning has an eerie peacefulness. I almost expect to see beady eyes, illuminated by my headlamp, making their way toward me. Only the mesmerizing dripping of water falling from my paddle can be heard. I am pleased with the intimacy of the Atchafalaya.

In less than an hour, the dark curtains of night open, revealing a golden sky and a promising new day. I put my headlamp away and absorb the unique features of the Atchafalaya River. As the riverbanks lower, some houses are elevated on stilts. Canals make their way through openings in the vine-tangled trees, connecting the river to massive swamps. I remember the Cajun guys' warning, "Whatever you do, stay on the main channel. So many people get lost wandering in the bayous." Because of my scheduled meeting with my wife and son tomorrow, I don't venture away from the main channel.

During the morning hours, I pass the Louisiana towns of Melville and Krotz Springs. Rust, caused by humidity and frequent precipitation, age the bridges that cross the river. They look as though, at any minute, they will crumble and fall into the Atchafalaya.

Clouds fill the sky, spurring me to paddle with determination. My GPS registers 5.2 miles per hour. I put away mile after mile.

I never imagined I could feel safer than I did on the Mississippi River. I don't have to look for the fastest and safest route, as the current is more constant and predictable. Even though the rivers are comparable in color and clarity, less debris clutters the Atchafalaya River. Barge traffic is significantly less; I've passed only one, so far. Fewer dangers give me more room to progress farther, faster.

Early afternoon, two teenage boys fish from a small barge parked near a bend in the river.

"Where you going?" one asks, as they both stand to get a better look.

"Morgan City," I respond. I maneuver my boat as the current tries taking me into the cables anchoring the barge.

"Where you from?" the other boy asks.

"Wisconsin." They look at each other, mouths gaping. As I zip around the tow, they run to the other side watching me as I disappear from their view around the curve.

During the afternoon hours, I see several johnboats hauling men dressed in camouflage. In some boats, bow-hunting gear is visible. At times I hear shots fired from rifles and shotguns. This area seems to be a popular hunting spot.

Soon the sun will be setting, so I begin scouting for a campsite—my final campsite of the expedition. *My last night; I can't believe it.* There were some days when I thought this trip would never end and now I'm looking for one last place to set up my tent.

Just when I think I've found a place that will do, a "PRIVATE" OR "NO TRESPASSING" sign forces me to keep moving. Forty minutes before sunset, a small rim of dry ground emerges on the west riverbank. With no signs visible, I pitch my tent about fifteen yards from the river's edge. Ten yards behind the tent is swamp—as far as I can see. I'm not a hundred percent sure the land isn't private, so I haul my kayak and all my gear into the woods, so as not to be seen by a passerby.

After a quick supper, I check the maps and GPS for daily mileage. *Wow! Sixty miles—my longest paddle yet.* My back and butt agree with the calculations.

I sit with my legs hanging out of my tent. I look out at the Atchafalaya like I did so many nights on the Mississippi. The river flows silent, smooth. Hoot owls sound off in the woods. The symphony of chirping crickets crescendos as the evening light dims. An occasional white egret skims gracefully over the water. *Maybe it's looking for a place for the night. Maybe it's heading home, as I will be soon.*

Day 42

N. 30° 10' 12"
W. 91° 31' 41"

My eyes pop open; my heart races. *Am I dreaming?* I glance at my watch; it's 12:30 a.m. *There it is again!* Branches and twigs snap. *No, I'm not dreaming.* It's not the snapping of twigs or the rustling of leaves that's so unusual, it's the breathing—the steady, slow, heavy breathing that this *thing* is making. My mind races trying to identify what it is—*whatever it is, it sounds very large.*

I lay silent, almost paralyzed by its breathing. It makes its way toward my tent, through the dense bayou thickets. I rise up slowly, ever so quietly, my hand reaching for my knife. Careful not to make any sudden movement or loud noises, I reach for my headlamp and place it on my head. In one swift motion, I quietly exit my sleeping bag and sit still in a kneeling position.

The *beast* approaches to within six feet of my tent. *Now you've invaded my comfort zone, buddy!* Only two thin sheets of nylon separate us; my breathing becomes shallow, trying to silence my deafening heartbeat. *I don't want to have to confront you.* Deciding I need to do something, I turn on my headlamp, hoping my glowing tent will frighten it away.

I yell out in a commanding voice, "Hey, what's going on out there?" *What do you say to an unknown creature that doesn't speak your language?* I pause, listening for a response. The deep, hideous breathing stops, as well as its forward progress. For almost sixty long seconds I hold my breath. My hand clenches my knife. W*hat are you thinking, Beast? What's your next move?*

My brain is much more advanced—able to reason. I have nothing to fear. As I'm giving myself a pep talk, the *thing* moves slowly, unafraid…in the opposite direction. I listen till it moves out of hearing range. I take in a deep breath, like a dead man coming to life. My heart slowly returns to it normal rhythm.

This little episode reminds me of a similar situation in the Alaskan bush.

During a fly-in moose hunt, my brother and I pitched our tent on the tundra in wolf and grizzly country. During the night, an animal approached our fragile shelter. That night we didn't reach for our knives; rather we gripped our guns. But by the time we got up enough nerve to poke our heads out the tent door, whatever it was, was gone.

I return to my sleeping bag, listening, making sure it really has left my vicinity. Slowly, I relax, convinced I will never see or hear from it again. I gradually drift off to sleep.

My eyes popped open again. A branch snaps close by. I check my watch; it's 3:30 a.m. *Now what?* This last night has been anything but the peaceful, restful night I had envisioned.

The swamp environment surrounding my small tent falls silent. My ears strain for the slightest sound. *Is it the same creature that visited my camp earlier? There, another sound—softly this time.* Once again, I rise up in my sleeping bag. Slow, deliberate, quiet steps pass between my tent and kayak. Another set of steps follows behind the first. *These are not the same sounds I heard earlier.* Confident the noisemakers are deer, I remain motionless—listening. I don't feel the need to reach for my knife or headlamp this time. In minutes, the visitors leave. I lay down for the second time, hoping the rest of my night is uninterrupted.

My eyes pop open once again. This time it isn't because of sounds of nature, but rather the bittersweet anticipation of the final day of my solo expedition. It is 5:15 a.m., on October 15, in the Atchafalaya River Basin. Before jumping out of my sleeping bag and attacking the day, I listen. It is as if all nature pauses with me, awestruck by this momentous occasion.

A half-hour later I slip into my loaded kayak. Looking toward heaven, brilliant stars light up the Louisiana sky. I thank God for equipping me with strength and providing me with protection each day of this incredible journey. He has shown me a glimpse of His greatness evident in His creation that surrounds me everyday. I start off in the still, cool darkness of the Atchafalaya River Basin.

It isn't until about 7:30 a.m. that the sun shows itself in rich oranges. Shortly after tucking my headlamp away, a boat motors downriver behind me. I paddle toward shore to allow the craft to pass without having to swing around my kayak. The engines cut to an idle a hundred yards behind. I stop paddling as the boat approaches. The engines quit altogether.

"Where'd you come from?" a voice calls from the cabin window.

"Wisconsin."

"What?" the voice exclaims.

"Yes, sir. I've paddled 1,650 miles to get this far," I explain. Two men, silhouetted against the golden sky, climb onto the deck.

"You're kidding? You came all this way in that?"

Before I can answer the man in the hard hat asks, "Need any water? Pop?"

"Sure, I'll take a pop."

"Get him two," he orders. "He needs some caffeine to get him going." The man with the baseball cap disappears into the cabin. "Wish we had more to give you. We do have crackers and peanuts. Can we give you some?"

The man in the baseball cap returns and hands me the two cans of cold Coca-Cola.

"Thanks for the Cokes. These are all I need."

The two men, who operate amphibious equipment for gas and oil companies, wish me luck and congratulations as they motor away slowly. Waiting for their wake to smooth, I drink one Coke, while it is still cold and for quick energy, and stash the other for later. Realizing I have several miles to cover to reach Morgan City and less daylight hours to do it in, I don't delay.

The sun inches it's way up the canvas of the sky painting over the oranges and golds with a brilliant blue. Not one cloud enters the picture. Only vapor wisps lurk in the shadows of the shaded shoreline.

At 9:00 a.m. I come upon a fisherman checking his lines.

"Good morning, sir," I say.

"Morning," comes his simple reply.

"You must be a commercial fisherman."

"Yes." As I glide alongside his boat, he reaches down with a large, weathered hand and gently holds the bow of my kayak. "Where you from?" he asks with a calm demeanor.

"Wisconsin." I answer Hagan's many questions about where I'm headed and why, what I carry and what I eat.

Hagan has been fishing this river since he was about eighteen years old. When I ask him if anyone helps him fish, his sad, yet understanding, eyes look down. His young-adult son helps him whenever possible, but mostly Hagan fishes the river alone. I could appreciate his loneliness. For several minutes Hagan freely shares about his life, shaped primarily by the Atchafalaya River.

Hagan's boat is interesting—different from any I have seen. Over the years he has customized his craft so that he can operate his engine and manipulate his nets from one spot at the front of the boat. Most fishermen's johnboats are operated from the stern, which means a second person needs to help pull in the nets, or a single fisherman would have to move between motor and nets.

Hagan's holding box is full of catfish. I am unable to see inside, so he offers to take a picture with my camera. The large fish bring only twenty-five cents a pound, whereas the smaller catfish are more valuable.

I could have talked for hours with Hagan, this simple fisherman with a gentle spirit and callused hands, but we both have to be on our way. He poses for a picture before releasing the bow of my kayak, returning me to my final day's journey.

The banks of the river are almost flat now. The shoreline is obscured by vegetation. It seems as though the river and swamp are running together. At times, large bogs covered with purple flowers become separated from the banks. Long vines latch on to the bogs, but the strong current breaks their hold, setting some of the bogs afloat.

As the riverbanks give way to the never-ending swamp, groves of cypress trees, adorned with beautiful, hanging moss, creep closer to the river's edge. Excited to finally behold these landmarks of the bayous from the seat of a kayak, I am mesmerized by their grandeur.

Soon I am jolted back to reality as the bayou yields its serenity to the hustle and bustle of Morgan City, Louisiana, a port

The Gulf Coast at last; my view of Morgan City, Louisiana.

town for Gulf operations. Barges, shrimp trawlers, oil tankers and other large ships motor about as I approach the outskirts of town.

The nostalgia of completing my 1,700-mile journey is obscured by an urgency to reunite with my family in a town unfamiliar to us all and before the sunsets. With barely two hours of daylight left, I recall the plan Wendi and I had agreed upon months before my quest began, of utilizing the Coast Guard as our means of connecting with one another. I flag down the first small boat coming toward me and ask the pilot for directions to the Coast Guard station.

"Well, it's a ways down river, yet. Do you see that train bridge?" He points downstream. "Go past the bridge and turn left onto the inter-coastal waterway. It's the fourth building on the left."

I paddle forward, feeling insignificant as I pass more ships that tower over me. The roaring of the channel dredging and clanging of ship work try to chase away the pilot's directions I locked into memory. With the bridge a mile or two ahead, my eyes scour the left bank in hopes of spotting our white pickup truck Wendi will be driving, eliminating the need to continue to the Coast Guard station.

A long, cement wall divides the docking area from the town. A gate hangs over an opening in the wall, ready to block stormy waves from crashing into the town. Because I sit so low in the water, I can't see more than the top half of the buildings that line the street that leads down to the dock. "MORGAN CITY," is painted in block lettering on the wall to the south of the opening. A dock made of heavy-duty wooden beams runs along the front of the retaining wall. No sign of my reception party.

Needing to stick to the plan, I paddle on. Passing under the train bridge, I turn left onto a bayou canal. I look intently to my left—one, two, three, four. The fourth building is not the Coast Guard station; none of the buildings resemble a Coast Guard station.

I approach a man on a parked barge. "Sir, can you tell me where the Coast Guard Station is?"

"It might be over there." He points back the way I had just come. By the sound of his voice, he isn't very confident.

."I just paddled past there and didn't see any Coast Guard boats." I speak with urgency.

"Hold on a minute. I'll ask someone for you."

I float next to this metal behemoth, with its lowest deck ten feet above my head. Two men come to the side looking for someone.

"Hey!" I yell. "Down here!"

"Looking for the Coast Guard?"

"Yes."

"It's down the channel a ways yet, but you must go through a lock to get to it."

I thank the men and continue down the channel. I paddle on for another mile with no sign of the Coast Guard. It is now 4:15 p.m., and I am becoming agitated with vague directions that waste the precious little time I have left. With so much river traffic, this search could take hours. Time is running out, and I am physically and mentally drained from the pressure.

"I must stick to the plan," I mumble to myself. I turn around, deciding to go back to the Morgan City loading dock where I remember seeing a phone booth. Now paddling upstream, I dodge several barges, keeping alert for any large vessels that may cut off my passage at any moment.

The sun drops closer to the horizon. I reach the loading dock, physically exhausted from paddling more than fifty miles today, and mentally drained from chasing sketchy directions. My kayak bobs four feet below the dock. I grab hold of the beams and my weary arms lift my body to a precarious standing position. I place my hands on the dock and carefully swing one leg up, then the other, careful not to push my kayak away from the dock and out of reach. Turning on my belly, I reach over the edge of the dock for the mooring rope on the bow of my kayak.

I secure the kayak and retrieve my fanny pack, stocked with money, phone cards, a small notebook and pencil, etc. Steadying my land legs under me, I stand for the first time today. I look around, amazed at the thought that I have reached my final destination, the Gulf Coast of Louisiana. This is as close as I can get, as gale force warnings and small craft advisories keep me from going into the Gulf waters themselves.

Returning to my mission, I find the phone booth near the opening in the retaining wall. As is often the case, the phone book is missing. I look around; there's no one to ask about phone numbers or directions or anything.

Why didn't I think of it sooner? I'll call the Coast Guard on my VHF radio. Not wanting to use channel 16, as it is reserved for water emergencies, I try a different channel. I wait a minute. Nothing. I try another channel. Again, nothing. As I twist the knob to a third channel, something unbelievable happens—the crazy pay phone rings. Stunned by the miracle, I pick up the receiver on the fourth ring.

"Hello?" I say with suspicion in my tone.

"Hi! How you doing?" a voice asks.

"I'm not sure I'm the person you're looking for," I respond.

"Hi. My name is Eddy."

"Hi, Eddy. My name is Byron."

"Hi, Byron. What brings you down here?" After giving him the rundown of my trip in a nutshell, he responds, "Wow! You must be really tired?"

"I am and I'm trying to connect with my wife and son who are coming to Morgan City to pick me up. I was going to call the Coast Guard, but I don't have a phone book to look up the number.

"I have a phone book right in front of me. I'll look the number up for you."

Wow! I can't believe this is happening! What perfect timing. Maybe he's an angel—Angel Eddy.

Eddy gives me a number, then offers, "I'll be coming down that way in about an hour. If you're still there, I can give you a ride somewhere."

I would like to meet Eddy, but at the same time, I'm hoping to be swept away by my wife and son in a small white pickup truck and delivered to a motel room with a comfortable bed and a hot shower.

I drop the change into the phone and dial. It rings once, twice. "U.S. Coast Guard."

"Sir," I begin, "I'm a kayaker that has paddled from Wisconsin to Morgan City. I'm supposed to meet my wife here. Has she checked in with you?"

The moment of silence seems forever. My heart pounds in anticipation.

"Yes," he responds, "about ten minutes ago." He promptly gives me the motel phone number Wendi left with the station.

I quickly dial the number using my calling card; my hands shake from sheer excitement. With each ring, my heart pounds harder. *Come on. Answer!* After five long rings, I hear the most soothing voice.

"Hello?" I could hear the disbelief in her tone.

"Hi, Honey. I'm in Morgan City."

"I just got off the phone with the Coast Guard a few minutes ago. I didn't expect to hear from you so soon. Where are you?"

"I'm on the dock in front of the retaining wall. "MORGAN CITY" is painted in big letters on the wall."

"I know exactly where you are. I saw the wall when I crossed the bridge into town. I'll be there in five minutes."

We hang up the phone so quickly, I can't remember if we said, "Good-bye."

I return to my kayak with a bounce in my step. A large houseboat, with twenty-some red gas cans tied to the deck, has nestled up behind my kayak. *I hope my kayak's still there.* Two men stand on the dock, looking down into the water.

"My kayak in your way?" I ask.

"Oh, no." Then one asks the infamous question. "Where did you come from?"

"Prescott, Wisconsin."

"Well, we came from Stillwater," he says with enthusiasm. Stillwater, Minnesota, is situated on the St. Croix River, north of Prescott. "We came right through Prescott."

"Imagine that. You're an original Tom Sawyer. You paddled all that way!" exclaims the second man. "That's really a trip."

The first man disappears and the second busies himself on the deck of his houseboat. I lay belly down on the dock to unload the contents of my kayak onto the dock. As I reach down for the last of my gear, I hear a faint whisper behind me. I jump up like a flash and whip around. Wendi, Isaac and I stare at each other for a few seconds. With two quick steps, I cover the distance between us. I reach for both of them, pulling them in for a long hug. After forty-two days we are reunited again.

We load the kayak onto the racks and deposit all my weathered and worn gear into the bed of the truck. Before leaving, one of the houseboat owners offers to take a picture of three very happy faces. He hands my camera back to me and turns to Isaac.

"Son, do you realize what your father has done?"

Isaac looks intently at the man.

"Your dad is an original Tom Sawyer. He paddled down that river and accomplished something great. You can be proud of that, Son. I saw two Navy Seals paddling down the river in a canoe. Your dad did it all by himself. That is a great accomplishment," he repeats.

He turns to me and says, "I have something for you." He steps into the cabin of the houseboat and returns shortly, carrying something in his hand. He presents a cap with gold bars on the bill and "River Rat" embroidered on the hat.

"You really earned this. You have done something few men will ever do." He shakes my hand. At this moment I feel as though I have been summoned to the stage in front of a large crowd, where someone of importance stands, waiting to congratulate me with a handshake and a medal of honor. What a ceremonious ending to my river quest.

Before leaving, we pause a moment to pray, thanking God for bringing us back together as a family and for the safety He showered over me as I traveled from the bluffs of Wisconsin to the bayous of Louisiana.

Morgan City

N. 29° 41' 14"
W. 91° 11' 39"

CONCLUSION

There is so much water that needs exploring, whether it's near home or thousands of miles away. It doesn't matter if it's been explored by others before; it needs to be explored by you. Don't just dream about it; get out there and make your own "water trail".

I hope that someday this book finds its way into the hands of my grandchildren and beyond. May they experience the joys of paddling and appreciate God's creation as I have. If it is still possible, my desire is that they plan an expedition of their own, or maybe follow my journey down the Mississippi and Atchafalaya Rivers camping at some of the same places I did. To future generations, I leave the legacy of this trip.

EPILOGUE
2002 Team Eye to Eye
World Record Swim

Only two weeks have passed since returning home from my river trip when I receive a request by email. A Slovenian swimmer is looking for three kayakers to guide him down the entire length of the Mississippi River from its headwaters in Lake Itasca, Minnesota, to Mile Zero at the Head of Passes in the Gulf of Mexico—2,360 miles. Martin Strel will be attempting a world record for the longest distance ever swum, breaking his own long distance world record swimming the Danube River in Europe.

Guy Haglund, U.S. coordinator for Team Eye to Eye, who knew of my kayak trip down the Mississippi and Atchafalaya Rivers, arranges for me to meet Martin Strel. Intrigued, I drive to Guy's home in St. Paul, Minnesota, one weeknight in October 2001.

Martin, forty-seven years old, is only a few inches taller than me, but has a considerably larger build. Don't be fooled by my description. There are no rippling chest and stomach muscles or bulging biceps. More so, he resembles a bear, building up fatty reserves for an incredibly long swim down the Mississippi. In his best, broken English, Martin, a jolly fellow, asks me to join his team.

The birthplace of the Mississippi River, and the start of the Eye-to-Eye Project. Author with son, Isaac.

During the next week, I contemplate the commitment involved in such an expedition. I remember the long days of paddling and the endless twists and turns in the river from my own journey just days ago. I recall the storms that chased me off the river and the exhaustion I felt battling the wind and waves. Images of a lowly, red kayak dodging barges and ships, longer than the length of several football fields, flood my mind. *Do I really want to do this again? So soon?* After much deliberation and encouragement from my wife, I join the navigation team, along with Matt Mohlke from Oronoco, Minnesota, who paddled the entire Mississippi River in 1999 by canoe; and David Hale from Minneapolis, Minnesota, an expedition canoeist of Canada's remote rivers.

On July 4, 2002, with a ceremony and a small, but warm send-off, we, the kayakers, charge off after Martin Strel down the flooded waters of the Mississippi. We were not instructed as to the specifics of our job; all we know is that we are to guide Martin down the river. We trusted that we will learn as we go.

It is a challenge, at times, to communicate with Martin. His English is limited, and we can't speak one word of Slovenian. Early in the trip, when the river is narrower, shallower and littered with logs and rocks, we blow our whistles to warn of danger below the surface. Later, we retire our whistles and raise our hands or paddles to get Martin's attention. Day-by-day, as Martin's English vocabulary increases, our sign language becomes more refined.

Our number one job is keeping Martin safe. We situate our kayaks in a triangular formation—one on each side of him and the third either leading or trailing. Martin gauges his direction

One of the ocean ships that use the river below Baton Rouge, Louisiana.

by watching our kayaks. Each time he comes up for air, he looks, for the majority of the time, at the kayak to his left, staying six to ten feet from its side. Wherever we paddle, Martin follows.

Keeping Martin safe also means steering him clear of obstacles in the water, such as floating debris, as well as the vast variety of commercial and pleasure boats sharing the river. With a VHF marine radio I keep in contact with the barges and tows on the river, letting them know of our presence and asking for the best route for safe passage.

Each day is filled with river challenges, some new, some that repeat themselves daily. One challenge that worries us is inclement weather. It doesn't seem to bother Martin to swim through a severe thunder and lightning storm until we have a very close call. At about mile 61.7, before Cape Girardeau, Missouri, heavy rains pelt us, reducing visibility to only ten yards. I am on Martin's right, Matt is on his left and David trails behind. Even though the storm is raging and the three of us are very uncomfortable with the situation, we hold our formation around Martin, guiding him. Suddenly, a green buoy marker appears in front of me. I make a split second decision to pass on its left, putting myself between Martin and the buoy. Lightning flashes after I pass the buoy. We instinctively duck our heads.

"Lightning just struck the buoy!" David yells.

Martin is lifted and shoved ahead by the blast.

"Buoy catch lightning," Martin says.

I am glad the *buoy* caught the lightning and *I* didn't. Unanimously, the kayakers agree it is time to get off the water.

According to Martin, our number one job is to find the current. This, of course, helps him to swim faster, thus making more miles per day. We learn to guide him close to every third to

After 68 days, Martin Strel and the entire Eye-to-Eye Team set a new world record. Mile 0, the Head of Passes of the Mississippi River.

fifth buoy, so that he can judge the speed of the current. However, we do not want to be responsible for his death, so we always choose the safest route even if it means sacrificing a little current. We always do our best, whether he thinks so or not.

As this world record expedition progresses, we three kayakers become an inseparable team. We work together at all times, never becoming self-centered or lackadaisical. Every minute, hour and day we are focused on the finish that lay ahead of us.

We struggle at times with fatigue and the stresses that are involved in a project so intense. However, our problems on the river are different from those of our ground crew. A motor home and van follows, providing food and communication support just when we need it. But as we progress farther south, timely assistance becomes a great struggle and challenge for them. Some roads on the map no longer exist, forcing the ground crew to drive many miles out of their way to get to us. A huge thanks goes out to them, for our trip could end prematurely if not for their perseverance.

Each day Martin Strel, marathon swimmer, amazes us. Swimming anywhere from ten to thirteen hours each day, he never wavers from his goal, even though pain in his arms, legs and back increase and deprive him of much needed sleep. On one occasion, Martin is very sick for three consecutive days. We anticipate that he will quit, or at the very least, take a day off. Instead he swims despite the misery. Martin is a champion; his daily focus and determination can be a lesson to us all.

As we approach the mile zero marker, we all raise our paddles. Martin stops and looks up. "Is this it?" he asks.

I answer, "Yes, Martin. Mile zero. The finish."

"The finish?" he asks again.

"The finish, Martin."

"Can't believe!"

He calls for us to join him near the dilapidated wooden structure that holds up a neglected and leaning sign that reads, "MILE 0." We pose arm in arm and Martin waves both the Slovenian and American flags. We are triumphant! And yes, it is hard to believe!

A new world record is established in sixty-eight days. I am honored to be a part of this incredible accomplishment. Congratulations to Martin Strel and the whole Eye-to-Eye Team. The seemingly impossible is possible.

2001 SOLO EXPEDITION GEAR LIST

Kayak Equipment
Kayak -
Current Designs Gulfstream
Paddles -
Werner Camano 220
Werner Little Dipper 220
Life jacket
Spray skirt
Paddle float
Bilge Pump
Rescue stirrup
Mooring rope
Cockpit cover
Dry bags
Deck bag
Multi-tool
Sponge

Navigation
GPS - Garmin etrex
VHF marine radio
Binoculars
Maps and map case
Compass

Safety Equipment
Flares
First aid kit
Whistle
Emergency blanket

Camping Equipment
Tent
Sleeping bag
Sleeping pad
Headlamp and bulbs
Knife
Multi-fuel stove
2 fuel bottles - 1 qt. each
Sunscreen
Bug repellent
1 cook pot
Utensils
3 Dromedary water bags
1 Nalgene bottle - 1.5 qt.
Water filter
Purification tablets
Matches and lighter
Miscellaneous toiletries

Clothing
Water shoes
Rain jacket and pants
Fleece Wind Stopper jacket
Fleece vest
2 hats
1 pair paddling gloves
5 pairs socks and underwear
4 pants - 3 zip-off
1 pair shorts
5 shirts - 3 long-sleeve

2001 SOLO EXPEDITION GEAR LIST (Cont.)

Food

6 lbs. rice
12 serv. instant potatoes
12 serv. oatmeal
6 serv. Cream of Wheat
Cheese
3 - 6 oz. powdered eggs
2 pkgs. dried refried beans
4 tuna pouches
5 bagels
10 tortillas
18 oz. peanut butter
16 oz. honey
2.5 cups powdered milk
15 chicken bullion cubes
15 beef bullion cubes
5 sauce packets
3 lbs. trail mix
3 lbs. dried apricots
Sport drink powder
2 Crystal Light powder
21 Power Bars
10 pkgs. hot cocoa
1 bag Snickers candy bars
2 oz. Molly McButter
Salt and pepper
Pkgs. condiments

Other

Camera
10 rolls film
Money
Phone cards
Personal identification
Kayak registration
2 Journals
5 mechanical pencils
Duct tape
Small diameter rope

RECOMMENDED MANUFACTURERS AND PADDLESPORT SHOPS

People often ask me about the kayaks and paddles I use. Below are two manufacturers I highly recommend:

Current Designs Kayaks

HEAD OFFICE:
Current Designs
Unit 300
770 Enterprise Crescent
Victoria, B.C. V8Z 6R4
Phone: (250) 479-0106
Website: www.cdkayak.com

USA:
We-No-Nah
PO Box 247
Winona, MN 55987
Phone: (507) 454-5430
Website: www.wenonah.com

Werner Paddles

PO Box 1139 / 33415 SR 2
Sultan, WA 98294
Website: www.wernerpaddles.com

Two great places in the Midwest to purchase kayaks, canoes and gear are as follows:

Midwest Mountaineering

309 Cedar Avenue South
Minneapolis, MN 55454
Phone: (612) 339-3433
Website: www.midwestmtn.com

Rutabaga: The Paddlesport Shop

[illegible]20 West Broadway
Madison, WI 53716
Phone: (608) 223-9300
Website: www.paddlers.com